Praise for J. P. Hansen and *The Bliss List*

"In my capacity as a career advice columnist, I occasionally come across an expert resource that make my job of providing my readers with information easy. One such person is J. P. Hansen."

—Dr. Mark Goulston, *Los Angeles Times*

"*The Bliss List* is a must-read for anyone navigating the job market at any age. From résumé tips and practice interview questions to advice on how to channel positivity into your life, Hansen covers everything you need to know in an interesting and easy-to-read guide."

—Emily Driscoll, FoxBusiness Personal Finance Writer

"The Ambassador of Bliss gives perfect advice for all professionals. J. P. Hansen will have you searching your soul, believing in your abilities and sprinting down the path in pursuit of your bliss.

"In *The Bliss List*, J.P. breaks the mold when it comes to career books. Sure, there's salient advice on résumés, interviews and working with recruiters, but this book is so much more. It's inspirational. It's liberating. J.P. clearly understands the human spirit and cares about his readers. It's a career-transforming, life-changing must-read."

—Jeff Beals, award-winning author of *Self Marketing Power: Branding Yourself as a Business of One*

"J. P. Hansen's book *The Bliss List* helps the reader navigate the world of work and find career opportunities that will ignite their passions and make going to work an exciting adventure."

—Chris Policinski, CEO, Land O'Lakes

"*The Bliss List* is more than a book about careers. It is a practical guide and an enjoyable read, where Hansen takes you down the path to real happiness in your work and life."

—Shoya Zichy, award-winning author of *Career Match: Connecting Who You Are With What You'll Love To Do* and *Women And The Leadership Q*

"People come up to me all the time and say 'I always wanted to write a book' or 'I always wanted to do a radio talk show' and I always ask them the same question . . . 'Why don't you?' Too many people limit themselves from what they really want out of life. They put up obstacles that prevent them from being who they really want to be. They talk themselves out of getting that dream job. *The Bliss List* helps motivate, inspire, and train people to follow their dreams. Some people say that life is too short. Personally I believe that life is too long for you not to be following your own individual bliss."

—Tom Becka, Top 20 Radio Personality and author of *There's No Business Without the Show! Using Showbiz Skills to Get Blockbuster Sales!*

"*The Bliss List* has really changed my job search around! I have landed over five interviews with some pretty great companies, and they all look very promising. I will continue to recommend your book to everyone I know getting out of the Army or contemplating making a career move. Thanks again for all of your help and I look forward to talking to you again."

—Jon Williamson, Captain, U.S. Army

"*The Bliss List* drastically changed my perspective on my career advancement. I came back to work with a new attitude and a spirit of gratitude. I would highly recommend the book to others. [It] has been my gift of choice for birthdays, anniversaries and 'just because I was thinking of you.' I can only imagine how much more productive we can be as an organization if the associates were happy!"

—Wendy R. McSweeney, Vice President, Wells Fargo

THE
Bliss List

THE

Bliss List

Discover What Truly Makes You Happy—
Then Land Your Dream Job

J. P. HANSEN

Reader's
Digest

The Reader's Digest Association, Inc.
New York, NY / Montreal

ISBN: 978-1-62145-092-4
Library of Congress Control Number: 2009930144

The Library of Congress has catalogued the original edition as follows:
    Hansen, J. P. (James Parker)
        The bliss list : the ultimate guide to living the dream and beyond / J. P. Hansen. – 1st ed.
        xii, p. ; cm. *
        Includes index and acknowledgments.
        ISBN 978-0-9840934-1-0 (pbk.)
        ISBN 0-9840934-1-9 (pbk.)
    1. Job hunting. 2. Career changes. 3. Career development.
    HF5382.7.H36 2009
    650.14 – dc22   2009930144

We are committed to both the quality of our products and the service we provide to our customers. We value your comments so please feel free to contac us.
    The Reader's Digest Association, Inc.
    Adult Trade Publishing
    44 South Broadway
    White Plains, NY 10601

For more Reader's Digest products and information, visit our website:
    www.rd.com (in the United States)
    www.readersdigest.ca (in Canada)

Printed in the United States of America

10 9 8 7 6 5 4 3 2 1

This book is dedicated to the loving memory of my mother, Mary C. Hansen.

CONTENTS

Introduction
The Secret of Success

"The secret of success is to make
your vocation your vacation."
Mark Twain

Did you pick up this book because you are unhappy in your current job? Do you want more from your work and from life? You are not alone. We all want bliss in our lives! America is in the midst of a crisis—a workplace crisis.

According to recent statistics, and backed up by my own experience of almost 20 years as a successful executive recruiter: Four out of five people are unhappy in their current jobs!

That's 80 percent! Why is this?

Part of the answer is what we can learn from that fifth person who is "happy" in his or her current job. If you are part of the 80 percent who are unhappy, this book will definitely help you; if you are part of the 20 percent who are happy, this book will help you in unexpected ways, either by enhancing your current job or leading you to a new one.

The Bliss List will help you discover your bliss, then get you into your bliss zone, then harness it, and, finally, make your bliss actionable for your vocation—and life.

What could cause an unhappiness rate of 80 percent? For the past 25 years, corporate America has been through a significant number of downsizings, mergers and acquisitions (another phrase for downsizing,) and bankruptcies. Every time a consultant is hired by a company, the "advice" inevitably results in layoffs. I have worked for four companies prior to starting my own company. Every single company for whom I worked either sold outright or divested the entire division that I was in.

I know I'm not alone. For the last 20 years, I have owned an executive search business, and it often seems as if it is an outplacement center, given all of the people I speak with just after being downsized (a nicer way to say, "You're fired!"). It is hard to find attitudinal bliss in the workforce when you are living under a constant threat of being canned.

On a somewhat deeper level, one of the main causes of unhappiness is society. Think about it. Let's say you will live to the age of 80. Where do you spend most of your time? If you said "sleeping," give yourself a pat on the back (or, better yet, a nap). What is a close second? Working.

Sleeping and working: this really is your life. Take out two weeks for a vacation and you are spending 2,000 hours in any given year working. This assumes you *only* work forty hours per week. Add seven hours of sleep per night, and sleeping and working represent close to two-thirds of your time. Not much time is left for anything else.

The Bliss List will primarily focus on the number-one occupier of your waking time—your job. But the lessons you will learn will carry over into all facets of your life.

What does unhappiness in your job have to do with society?

You spent the first 18 or so years of your life with little or no work stress. Your parents took care of you—providing clothing, food, and shelter, and paying the tab for almost everything else. You slept even more than seven hours per day during childhood and could sleep all day during the teenage years (and on some days you did). You may have worked part-time jobs, but work stress was secondary.

Then you reached the cut-off point—the last year of school, whether it was high school, college, or graduate school. This is the "uh oh, what do I do now?" phase. And it's quick—too quick for most.

Your conditioning up to this point had been sleep, play, and study—with very little work.

Unless you are independently wealthy, you will work at least 86,000 hours in your lifetime (starting at age 22 and retiring at 65). Yet, the time spent deciding what to do is miniscule. Even if you tried to think ahead, it's not really possible to know what jobs are right for you until you've experienced the working world a bit. As graduation approached, you panicked, thinking "What am I going to do?" You had a lot of years to prepare, but no matter what guidance counselors told you, you didn't learn how to find a job that's truly right for you, namely following your bliss.

With the real world looming, the pressure on finding a job built. Your parents, who had been footing your bill, may have even mentioned the importance of finding a job. Thus, your first job was usually decided on a whim: "I'll go with whoever offers me the most money, or I'll take the first job I can get."

This is not exactly the most solid ground on which to make a great decision, let alone lead you to an ideal job. Is it any surprise that, at age 22, you didn't find a job you would love?

Are you one of these people? Be honest now. If you qualify, go easy on yourself. You are definitely not alone. But there is help. *The Bliss List* will teach you to stop living your life in default and to take control of your job (and life)—starting today. You can make things happen for yourself.

Why isn't there a course on seeking and finding your blissful dream job during your formal education phase? On average, you spend 18 years sitting in school without gaining much practical knowledge for the real world. It's no surprise, then, that a whopping 80 percent of us are unhappy once we hit the real world.

I know I didn't learn many useful job-seeking skills in school, but I feel I have attained the equivalent of a couple of advanced degrees since then through information I have devoured over the last 30 years. I have read hundreds of books, listened to hours and hours of CDs and tapes, and watched hours on end of DVDs/videos on mystical insights from many enlightened people throughout time. Add these to hundreds of books on business acumen from some impressive business geniuses.

Yet I have never read a book that put it all together for me. If you are going to spend an average of 86,000 hours working, there should be an all-in-one book to help you find bliss in that work and your life. This book will help you discover your dream job—the one at which time stands still for you. Then you will receive practical advice on how to obtain it.

DEFINING BLISS

Dr. Martin Luther King, Jr., said, "Take the first step in faith. You don't have to see the whole staircase. Just take the first step." Reading this book is the first important step toward reaching what so many of you are missing in life: bliss! Simply defined, *bliss* is happiness and meaning. My goal is to share insights with you. Some may seem controversial; some may rock your world. But after reading *The Bliss List,* you will grow personally and professionally. I guarantee it!

Congratulations on taking the first step. My promise is that after reading this book you will find bliss and land that elusive dream job. It may even be more than one vocation. I have worked for over 31 years in a wide variety of jobs. As an executive recruiter, I helped thousands of people find their bliss through their work for almost 20 years, and with this book I hope to help millions do the same.

You are always growing and obtaining new peaks (and experiencing some valleys). This book will help you reach new peaks that may have seemed unreachable before. And then to reach new ones. There will be no room for valleys from here on.

We are spiritual beings living in a physical presence. *The Bliss List* will combine the practical with the mystical. The advice you gain from this book—obtaining true joy from your work—will also help you transform your life in every area.

I have been blessed with good fortune throughout my career and life. My dreams have been realized many times. I graduated from Boston College, my first choice, and then obtained several dream jobs with blue-chip companies like Nestle, Bristol-Myers Squibb, SC Johnson Wax, and ConAgra. I worked with some very talented people and was lucky to have several mentors who "taught me the ropes," and who continue to help me.

I became a self-made millionaire by age 37. After being the youngest Vice President (at age 31) with a Fortune 35 company, I am now the president of a highly successful executive search company and have helped thousands of job seekers find true bliss. I owned a gorgeous dream house outright—that's right, with no mortgage. I owned a prime villa on beautiful Hilton Head Island outright. I owned a BMW outright.

The feeling of financial freedom was incredible, but it has not always been easy street for me. I have had my down years—my own valleys. But when I did, I bounced back. My experiences—good and bad—are real and captured in this book, so my book offers real-life, practical insight that will help you.

Applying Dr. Martin Luther King, Jr.'s belief that things happen in steps, the same was true for me in landing my ultimate dream job: owning my own business. Before I could obtain it, though, I knew I needed more training (and credibility). I have interviewed for several jobs and been the interviewer, plus I serve as a career coach in my role as an executive recruiter.

Along the way, I was able to obtain seven different dream jobs and some *not exactlys,* which ultimately gave me the experience and courage I needed to start my own company.

If you view your own bliss as a series of steps, you will constantly be in a dream job state, regardless of your occupation. You will always be living in ultimate bliss.

Though my career may seem like a cake walk, don't think it was easy. Every single company and/or division for which I worked was sold within the first year of my employment. Many people with whom I worked were pulled under by a wave of negativity. Nevertheless, I never allowed myself to sway from my belief that I would one day have my own business and live in financial prosperity.

TELL ME ABOUT YOURSELF

"Follow your bliss and doors will open
where there were no doors before."
Joseph Campbell

One of the many things I enjoy about being an executive recruiter is that I get to wear several hats in my job. One of those hats is psychologist. People pour out their hearts and share their inner secrets with me all the time. I have developed the skill of quickly determining whether someone is appropriate for a given job search I'm conducting.

I follow a simple but effective method: I start by giving a brief thumbnail sketch of my background in order to build credibility and gain the person's trust. This only takes a minute or two, but is very powerful. Trust is the key to a strong relationship. After I feel I've built enough trust, I ask for a brief synopsis of the person's background. Then, I shut up (not a natural thing for me) and listen—very intently.

I learn a great deal after asking the question, "Tell me about yourself." What the person answers reveals all that is important:

- How he or she feels about his or her background—a great barometer for future success (or failure in some cases)
- His or her energy level
- How well he or she verbalizes thoughts
- His or her basic interview skills—if you can't eloquently tell me about yourself, how can you ever do well in an interview?

After hearing the person's answer in describing his or her background, I always say, "Wow, you have a terrific background. What do you want to do next?" You would be amazed at how many people stumble at this basic question. If I had a dollar for every time a person replied, "I'm not sure . . . what have you got?" I would no longer need to work. Isn't this the essence of what is keeping a person from achieving bliss?

If you don't know what you want to do, how can you have a blissful dream job? Sometimes, the answer is, "Well, I know it isn't what I'm doing now!" This is actually an important step in obtaining bliss— by using contrast. Sometimes, you need to state what you don't want in order to decide what you do want. Using our previous examples of happiness and unhappiness, we can see that sometimes this contrast is needed to develop our true goals.

I'll tell you the story of Gary.

I bought a dream house not too long ago. Here, the word *dream* really works because it was in foreclosure and in need of some drastic repairs and major remodeling. Many people looked at the house and passed on it (they thought I was dreaming to think I could fix it up). As a result, my ultimate dream house was on the market for over a year. The house had so much potential, and I could visualize what it would look like with some creative improvements.

Gary worked for the general contractor I hired for this remodeling job. He used to run his own remodeling business but fell on hard times and a nasty client or two and decided he needed more security, so he went to work for someone else. Gary was competent. He had a can-do attitude. No matter what I asked—and some of my requests and ideas were extreme—Gary would always say with a proud smile, "I can do that!" And he was right.

Despite this outward optimism, Gary had an inner roadblock: he was not happy in life. One day, Gary asked me if I could help him find a job. Using my method, I asked him what he wanted to do next? He shot back, "Well, I don't want to be a carpenter!"

I paused, and then asked again, "What do you want to do?"

Gary retorted, "I don't want to be a carpenter."

Looking somewhat annoyed, I asked a third time, "What is it you *want* to do?"

Gary's third answer was the same, "I *don't* want to be a carpenter."

It was almost like the biblical story of the apostle Peter denying knowing Jesus three times before the cock crows. Gary was denying himself three times. I waited for a moment and didn't hear any cock crowing, but began asking Gary some different questions.

After a short while, he determined that he really wanted to be in business for himself again. And that he was passionate about carpentry, but wanted to be able to do a wider range of work. He wanted to be a general contractor capable of doing any project himself.

It was easy for me to encourage him after seeing all the outstanding things he had done in my remodeling project. I asked him what was holding him back.

He responded, "My wife would leave me if I did."

I asked, "Why?"

His excuse was "the money." I took out a sheet of paper and did some basic math, applying the economics of business ownership. The result was a no-brainer. On paper, he saw he would conservatively double his income in his own business. He was running out of excuses.

We spent about a half hour dispelling all of his excuses—limitations, roadblocks, and mind pollution—which were keeping him from obtaining his blissful dream job. They were rooted in fear—fear of failure.

Over the next month, Gary began focusing on starting (or rather, re-starting) his own business. He would ask me my opinion about ideas, but rather than give him my take, I would try to draw the answer out of him. He was really focused on starting his own company. I could sense his enthusiasm. His vision for his own dream job was developed through contrast. Saying what he didn't want to do had opened him up to what he really wanted—his passion.

It was only a matter of time before Gary was ready to take action. He had set his goal and was very enthusiastic, but still lacked confidence. I knew he needed to take action. Action drives results, and results build confidence.

I told him to print up some company cards and make lawn signs. For a small amount of money and time invested, he could see if he could drum up some business and prove to his skeptical wife that the money would be greater. He developed a company name, registered it as a corporation, and began focusing on his dream job.

In just a matter of weeks, he obtained a couple of lucrative contracts and voilà—he was on his own. He was so enthusiastic, I could feel it. He was a changed man. And it really was simple: he shifted his thoughts from what he didn't want (with fear and doubt) and turned to what he really did want (with enthusiasm and confidence), and his dream job became reality. His wife is even happy. Doubling his income over his first two months didn't hurt.

Gary is living the dream and loves his work. Gary found his bliss. Now let's help you find yours.

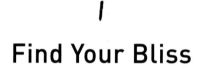

1

Find Your Bliss

*

"Nothing is more important
than reconnecting with your bliss.
Nothing is as rich. Nothing is more real."
Deepak Chopra

You already possess your inner bliss—your dream job. And you will likely have more than one. For you to find your blissful dream job, you have to firmly believe this. By reading this book right now, you are moving one important step closer to obtaining your dream job, and finding bliss in your life. Your bliss is literally right around the corner.

Actually, your bliss is inside of you. My goal is to help you truly look inside yourself in order to discover what inspires you. You'll also examine external factors that may have blocked you from your own inner wisdom and eliminate them.

I know this sounds good in theory, but let me give you an example of how easily this concept can be turned into reality. A life coach client of mine—we'll call her Marissa—was unhappy with life in general, including her current job. When I asked her why, all she could come up with was, "Maybe I'm just having a mid-life crisis."

The more I pressed Marissa for specifics, the more she kept repeating "mid-life crisis," as if it was her mantra. I said, "Be careful what you say—I'm afraid it's become your affirmation. There's no such thing as a *mid-life crisis*. But, the more you keep saying it, the more you believe it."

On the surface, Marissa was a bright, successful accountant with a CPA, earning decent money. She was in good shape—a bit on the thin side—and looked younger than her actual age of fifty-three. Both of her parents had passed away within the last two years and Marissa had inherited enough money so she wouldn't have to work. During the past year, she had gone through a bitter divorce that I knew had shattered her self-esteem. She wasn't sleeping and was relying on anti-depressants to get through each day. What she really needed was a double dose of bliss.

Much of Marissa's present was polluted with her past—her upbringing. Her fears began early. Marissa was raised to believe that *bliss wasn't possible until she died; that hell is on earth.* Blah, blah, blah—I've heard that one plenty of times. What a tragic way to live. I tried to fight fire with fire, quoting scripture: "The kingdom of heaven is within." When I asked her what that meant, she couldn't tell me. Marissa needed to reconnect with her own inner bliss.

My verbal efforts had been fruitless, so I asked Marissa to write down what she was grateful for and I left the room. This forced her to do some soul searching. Just thinking about what makes you grateful raises your spirits and I hoped it would help break Marissa out of her invisible fence.

After about fifteen minutes, Marissa called me back in the room. She had filled up half the page. She said she struggled at first, but once she wrote the first one—that she was grateful for her patience—it became easier. From there, plenty of other thoughts flooded onto her paper. Interestingly, none of them were work related. After "my patience," she listed possessions—her car, house, vacation home, etc.

Then she wrote about her relationships: her dogs, two friends, and a cousin. Finally, she listed interests like music (she was a gifted pianist with a terrific voice), photography, and writing (she was trying to write a novel).

When she read her notes, her mood brightened like a radiant sunrise. I said, "Congratulations! You've taken the most important step to finding bliss in your life—without having to die first."

Marissa furrowed her eyebrows, then said, "That's not bliss; that's just what I'm grateful for."

I retorted, "What's the difference?"

She paused for a moment, then said, "None, I guess."

I asked, "During a given day, how much time are you actually spending with the people on that list or doing the activities you just read?"

Marissa inhaled deeply, and said, "Not nearly enough."

I knew my point resonated inside her. I said, "You know how to break out of your depression. Devote time to the things and people you just listed. You're not having a mid-life crisis, you're having a bliss crisis. Now that you know what makes you grateful, practice, practice, practice. Be your bliss and bliss will follow. Every time."

It only took Marissa 15 minutes to begin turning her "mid-life crisis" into joy. Like Marissa, the first step toward attracting your bliss is to devote some time pondering your own bliss. Some may say that sounds selfish. I say it's actually more selfish to wander around loaded up on anti-depressants, complaining about life. First, determine the people and things that make time stand still for you. The next step is to stay in your zone—your bliss zone.

Are you ready for your own *Bliss List?*

YOUR *BLISS LIST*

It's time to do some honest soul searching, so let's take an assessment. You will assess your skills, your desires, and your goals. This is a vital step toward obtaining your bliss, whether at work or in your life.

Think of *The Bliss List* as your working diary—your personal guide to living the dream at work (and life). Keep notes with this book for easy reference.

For this important exercise, simply write down what makes you feel the happiest. It doesn't have to be work-related. What makes time stand still for you? This is your *Bliss List*. Is it living like a millionaire? Being your own boss? The security of a stable company? Skimming over a lake in a sailboat? Skiing down a mountain? Hiking in the wilderness? Reading a spellbinding book? You decide.

This list should come naturally to you and not take more than a few minutes for you to write. You will feel your mood actually improve as you think about, and write, this list. Whatever you write, the only rule is that you tell yourself what makes you happy—not what makes your spouse, family, boss, friends, clergy, or whoever happy. Don't place any limits on yourself.

I'll give you an amazing example of another person's list after you're done, but I don't want to sway you with it yet. This list needs to be your *Bliss List*. Write at least fifteen words and phrases now.

1. _____

2. _____

3. _____

4. _____

5. _____

6. _____

7. _____

8. _____

9. _____

10. _____

11. _____

12. _____

13. _____

14. _____

15. _____

As promised, here's an example: Jack Canfield, world-renowned author of the bestselling Chicken Soup for the Soul series, compiled his passion points in *The Passion Test* by Janet Attwood and Chris Attwood. This was his *Bliss List*:

1. Being of service to massive numbers of people

2. Having an international impact

3. Enjoying celebrity status

4. Being part of a dynamic team

5. Having a leadership role

6. Helping people live their vision

7. Speaking to large groups

8. Having an impact through television

9. Being a multimillionaire

10. Having world-class headquarters and support team

11. Having lots of free time

12. Studying with spiritual masters regularly

13. Being part of a spiritual leader's network

14. Creating a core group of ongoing trainers who feel identified with my organization

15. Having fun, fun, fun!

I use Jack Canfield's list for a reason. Jack is an enormously successful man who has had a positive influence on people around the world. And his list reflects that. I especially liked his number one: "Being of service to massive numbers of people." Wow!

The bestselling author Jose Silva wrote that if you could help two additional people in anything you desire, you greatly increase your chances of manifesting it. I think being of service to massive numbers of people qualifies—and Jack has done it. And continues to do it.

Does your list have a degree of challenge in it? Jack's certainly does. I'm not saying you must have Jack's list, but remember, your list has no boundaries or limits (neither did Jack's). The higher you set your goals, the greater your results. Don't short yourself on your *Bliss List*; challenge yourself. If you need to return to your *Bliss List* to add or modify any items, please do so before you continue reading.

Here's an example from a client of mine; we'll call her Maria.

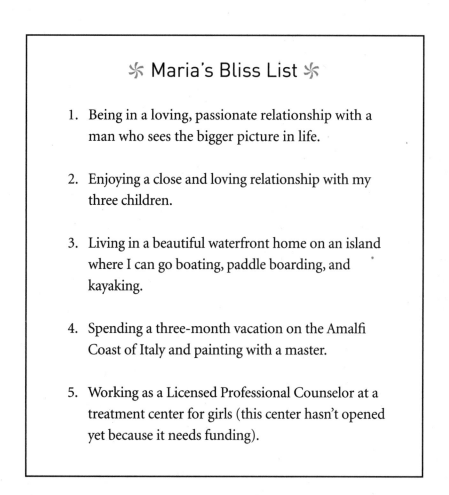

Maria's Bliss List

1. Being in a loving, passionate relationship with a man who sees the bigger picture in life.
2. Enjoying a close and loving relationship with my three children.
3. Living in a beautiful waterfront home on an island where I can go boating, paddle boarding, and kayaking.
4. Spending a three-month vacation on the Amalfi Coast of Italy and painting with a master.
5. Working as a Licensed Professional Counselor at a treatment center for girls (this center hasn't opened yet because it needs funding).

6. Having a leadership role as a therapist and as a teacher with families.

7. Giving people hope.

8. Being a part of a forward-thinking treatment team that believes in and implements positive psychotherapy.

9. Attending a weeklong workshop with a master of positive psychotherapy.

10. Having time for a great workout with weights and aerobics three times a week.

11. Owning a mountain house where I can ski in the winter.

12. Using my professional camera to capture the beauty of the world. Traveling with a famous photographer.

13. Walking my dogs on the beach every day.

14. Having a personal chef to cook healthy meals for me and for dinner parties with my friends.

15. Completing my LPC (Licensed Professional Counselor) certification.

Now that you have identified your bliss points, we'll cut it down to a top seven. Your brain functions like a computer: too many open applications slows down its effectiveness. Many scientists believe that the human brain functions best by handling only seven things at once. Use the space below to pare your previous list into the all-important *Top Seven Bliss List*:

1. _____

2. _____

3. _____

4. _____

5. _____

6. _____

7. _____

Post this list in plain sight (more on this later) and then tuck a copy in your wallet or purse too. This list is you. The more concentrated thought you put into this list with enthusiastic feeling and confidence, the quicker all seven will manifest in your life. I want you to go seven for seven here.

I asked Maria to rank her fifteen using her first impression (usually the right one to trust). Though she struggled to pare her list at first, here are her Top Seven bliss points:

❈ Maria's Bliss List Top Seven ❈

1. Being in a loving, passionate relationship with a man who sees the bigger picture in life.

2. Enjoying a close and loving relationship with my three children.

3. Living in a beautiful waterfront home on an island where I can go boating, paddle boarding, and kayaking.

4. Working as a Licensed Professional Counselor at a treatment center for girls (this center hasn't opened yet because it needs funding). Also, I am currently working on my LPC.

5. Having a leadership role as a therapist and as a teacher with families. Giving people hope.

6. Having time for a great workout with weights and aerobics three times a week.

7. Owning a mountain house where I can ski in the winter.

Next, we're going to apply your *Top Seven* into a first draft for your ideal job. You may have more than one ideal job—the more, the better (no limits, remember?). So, without further ado, you will simply write the title or titles of your dream job or jobs. Even if the title is fictitious, it doesn't matter; this is your blissful dream job after all. You may want to add a bit of a description to each title, but save the details for the next step. (You don't need to have exactly seven titles here—you could have more or less—this is just a starting point.)

1. _____

_____

2. _____

_____

3. _____

_____

4. _____

_____

5. _____

_____

6. _____

_____

7. _____

_____

Here's how Maria listed her dream job title:

❋ Maria's Dream Job Title ❋

Licensed Professional Therapist in a comprehensive treatment program that specializes in the personal empowerment, recovery resource development, evidenced-based treatment, support services, recovery, and advocacy for girls ages 12 through 17. This facility is on a beautiful piece of property where the girls will kayak and have access to an outdoor activity compound.

Now, write down a brief description of what each of these jobs entails. This should be as detailed as you can make it; the more vividly you can imagine them, the closer to reality they will be. Intersperse your *Top Seven* into it—they should be a match. Don't limit yourself to only salary. Think of what really makes you happy. The money will follow. What are you passionate about? Again, don't fret if it seems fictitious. The more you think of your dream jobs with enthusiasm and confidence, the more quickly fiction will turn into reality. (Again, you don't need to have exactly seven descriptions here, but can add more or have less, depending on your dream jobs.)

1. _____

   _____

2. _____

   _____

3. _____

   _____

4. _____

   _____

5. _____

   _____

6. _____

   _____

7. _____

   _____

Here's how Maria envisioned the tasks involved in her dream job:

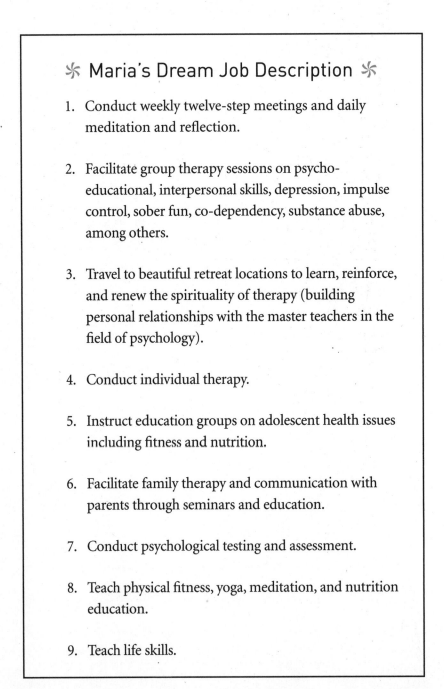

✳ Maria's Dream Job Description ✳

1. Conduct weekly twelve-step meetings and daily meditation and reflection.

2. Facilitate group therapy sessions on psycho-educational, interpersonal skills, depression, impulse control, sober fun, co-dependency, substance abuse, among others.

3. Travel to beautiful retreat locations to learn, reinforce, and renew the spirituality of therapy (building personal relationships with the master teachers in the field of psychology).

4. Conduct individual therapy.

5. Instruct education groups on adolescent health issues including fitness and nutrition.

6. Facilitate family therapy and communication with parents through seminars and education.

7. Conduct psychological testing and assessment.

8. Teach physical fitness, yoga, meditation, and nutrition education.

9. Teach life skills.

10. Facilitate organic gardening and culinary skills.

11. Teach photography and appreciation of nature and the beauty of the countryside.

12. Facilitate the expression of creativity and self expression through painting.

Next, write down what skills are necessary to do this job. Under this, write the skills you already possess. How does it match up? It probably is not too far off. (Again, use as much or as little space as you need here.)

Skills needed to do this job

1. _____

_____

2. _____

_____

3. _____

_____

4. _____

_____

5. _____

_____

6. _____

_____

7. _____

_____

Skills I already possess:

1. _____

_____

2. _____

_____

3. _____

_____

4. _____

_____

5. _____

_____

6. _____

_____

7. _____

_____

Here are Maria's lists of skills. Notice that she already possesses most of the skills she needs to do her dream job.

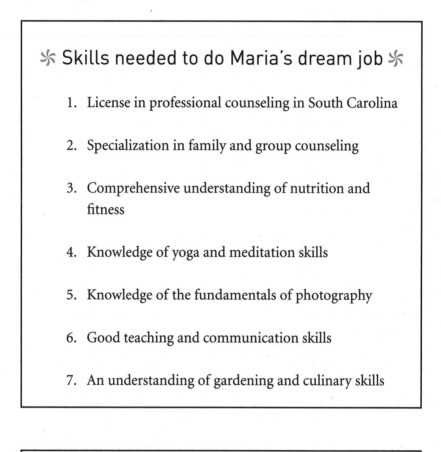

✴ **Skills needed to do Maria's dream job** ✴

1. License in professional counseling in South Carolina

2. Specialization in family and group counseling

3. Comprehensive understanding of nutrition and fitness

4. Knowledge of yoga and meditation skills

5. Knowledge of the fundamentals of photography

6. Good teaching and communication skills

7. An understanding of gardening and culinary skills

✴ **Skills Maria already possesses** ✴

1. Teacher for thirteen years

2. Comfortable presenting information

3. Masters in Education Counseling

4. Own and shoot a professional camera

5. Two yoga certifications

6. Workout five times a week and understand the fundamentals of fitness

7. Eat healthy and have a good understanding of nutrition

8. Good interpersonal skills

Finally, write down what steps are needed. If more education is required, list it. Will you need additional education/credentials like a certification? Would a degree, an additional class, a training seminar or merely a different company environment help you to obtain what is missing? Be as honest as possible and take no shortcuts (this means you may need more than seven steps, or you may need fewer). This is your dream job.

1. _____

_____

2. _____

_____

3. _____

_____

4. _____

_____

5. _____

_____

6. _____

_____

Here's what Maria needed to do:

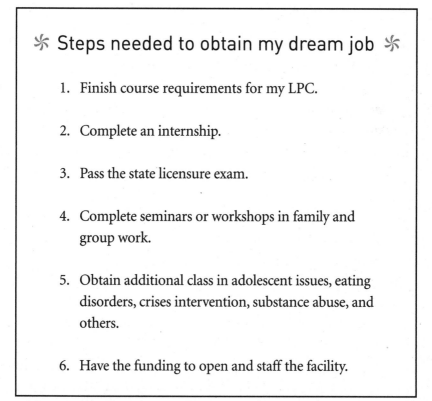

※ **Steps needed to obtain my dream job** ※

1. Finish course requirements for my LPC.

2. Complete an internship.

3. Pass the state licensure exam.

4. Complete seminars or workshops in family and group work.

5. Obtain additional class in adolescent issues, eating disorders, crises intervention, substance abuse, and others.

6. Have the funding to open and staff the facility.

TURN YOUR *BLISS LIST* INTO REALITY WITH BLISS CARDS

It's time to start amplifying your desires. Whether you believe in the Law of Attraction or think it's merely fantasy, I believe the more you think of something with enthusiasm and confidence, the more likely you are to manifest your goals in life.

The Law of Attraction went mainstream with the bestselling book and DVD *The Secret.* Some critics wrongly labeled it "New Age." The Law of Attraction is actually *age old,* predating the earliest writings of mankind. Divine manifestation has been practiced and studied by ancient (and wise) civilizations including Alexandria, Lemuria, and Atlantis. Plato and Aristotle understood and practiced these divine universal principles; Egyptian, Asian and Greek cultures were masters at divine manifestation. The Bible and the teaching of Buddha contain numerous references to this powerful law.

We live in a world where science and spirituality coexist, and even complement each other. This hasn't always been the case. The Law of Attraction is rooted in spirituality, but many elements have been scientifically proven through quantum physics.

In a nutshell, the Law of Attraction says that your thoughts (both conscious and unconscious) dictate the reality of your life, whether or not you're aware of it. Essentially, if you really want something and believe it's possible, you'll probably get it. Conversely, putting a lot of attention and thought into something you don't want means you'll probably get that too. Everything in your life can be explained by the Law of Attraction—good and bad.

For this practical application of the Law of Attraction, you simply need some 3- x 5-inch cards. These will be your Bliss Cards. Write your *Top Seven Bliss List* items on a card and keep it with you wherever you go: in your wallet/purse, pocket, dashboard of your car, on your refrigerator, and in your briefcase. You can also add some genius to your smart phone by adding your list on your wallpaper and screen savers, but physical cards are what have been scientifically demonstrated to work. The idea is to keep your list in a strategic place where you are most able to see it throughout the day. Look at it as often as you can. It is a very powerful tool in turning your *Bliss List* into reality.

After you have received one or more of the items on your *Bliss List,* simply save your card in a folder labeled "*Bliss List* Successes." Then make a new one.

Your *Bliss List* can change; in fact, you actually want it to change—and to grow. Remember, you are energy and are always moving. You will evolve, and so will your list. I update my list every three months or so, but it may vary for you.

Your *Top Seven Bliss List* on a simple Bliss Card is a powerful way to get the ball rolling on results. It has worked for me and for countless others. Well-known motivational speaker Bob Proctor (featured in *The Secret*) credits his enormous wealth to these cards. He carries one with his goals at all times.

I know you may be a little skeptical, but what do you have to lose? The cost for a few of these cards is pocket change but the return may be immeasurable—especially if it leads you to your bliss.

IN THE RIGHT FRAME OF MIND

Ever hear this phrase, "having the right frame of reference"? Or better yet, "putting yourself in the right frame of mind"? These little phrases are profound and hold an important key to obtaining your bliss in work and life.

"Reference point," for our discussion, means simply, emotions. If you are in a bad mood, guess what? Your point of attraction is bad, bringing you undesirable things. Conversely, if you are in a good mood, you will attract good, desirable things. There are two primary emotions: love and fear. They are polar opposites, and every emotion is a derivative of love and fear.

The following is an expanded basic reference point scale of emotions in order of most desirable to least:

1. Bliss/Enlightenment
2. Gratitude/Appreciation
3. Love
4. Happiness
5. Peace
6. Freedom
7. Knowledge
8. Empowerment
9. Positive Expectation/Belief
10. Optimism
11. Hopefulness
12. Contentment

~~~~~~~~~~~~~~~~~~~~~~~~~~~~~~~~~~~~

13. Boredom
14. Pessimism
15. Frustration/Impatience
16. Irritation
17. Disappointment
18. Doubt

19. Worry

20. Blame

21. Discouragement

22. Anger

23. Revenge

24. Hatred/Rage

25. Jealousy/Envy

26. Insecurity/Guilt/Unworthiness

27. Fear/Grief/Depression/Despair/Powerlessness

You are capable of feeling every single one of these emotional reference points. I have felt them all at one time or another. You have too. This is your ability to experience the full spectrum of emotions in life. This is the paradoxical concept of contrast: sometimes it takes feeling depressed to appreciate feeling happiness.

With the Law of Attraction, your attraction point is your emotional reference point. Prayer works this way, too. So does meditation. I know that to some people, meditation also sounds hokey or new age. But like Law of Attraction, meditation is age old. If you've ever said a prayer, it's a form of meditation that predates the Bible and even the teachings of Buddha. The terms "pray" and "meditate" are interchangeable and if you have trouble with the term "meditate," use "prayer" or "deep thought." Prayer is deep thought with feeling. See any metaphor for obtaining your blissful dream job? I hope so. If you pray from a negative point of reference (emotions on the list from 13 through 27), you will negate your prayer; from a positive reference point (using emotions from 1 through 12), your prayer will be answered.

Your point of reference needs to be in the positive area (emotions 1 through 12) if you are going to attract your bliss. The trick is getting there. It's not as hard as you may think. You control your point of reference. That's right, you can consciously choose to be in a loving, peaceful state, or you can choose to be upset with seemingly everything around you.

Remember, your bliss lies within you already. All you need to do is unlock it, find it, and follow it. Be in a positive frame of mind at least 95 percent of the time, and the majority of your results will be positive.

MAKING YOUR *BLISS LIST* WORK

The exercises you just completed were a very important step toward obtaining your blissful dream job. Just writing down your *Top Seven Bliss List* is powerful. It sets your goals in motion, and you will begin attracting what you intend with enthusiastic confidence every time.

There are ways you can make your *Top Seven Bliss List* work for you with more force, increasing its intensity (raising your vibrations). Remember, set your goal with enthusiasm and confidence. Writing the *Bliss List* is the start of your goal-setting. Developing the right frame of mind to receive your goal is equally important. Do the following:

- Review your *Bliss List* at least three times a day.
- Ask yourself, "Am I choosing a path that will lead me toward my *Bliss List* or away from it?" every time you are faced with a decision.

- Keep your frame of mind (emotional state) positive at least 95 percent of the time. If you stray, catch yourself, say "cancel," and think of something that makes you laugh.

- Meditate three times per day for 15 minutes (or do some other quiet activity such as prayer that brings you peace of mind).

- Develop an attitude of gratitude.

- Follow a healthy lifestyle that includes exercise and healthful foods.

- Think of your *Bliss List* in the present tense—as if it has already happened.

The more you can imagine your *Bliss List* has already happened (with confidence), the more likely you are to obtain that dream job.

Now, let's strengthen the list with a simple but highly effective exercise. Write out five measures of success that will happen when you are in your blissful dream job.

1._____

2._____

3._____

4._____

5._____

The following are some examples of my own measures of success for my dream jobs:

Bliss List: I am a famous author.

Measures of success:

1. I have been on *The New York Times* bestseller list.

2. I have reached over 1 million readers worldwide.

3. I earn over $1 million each year on book sales.

4. I have been interviewed on popular TV and radio shows.

5. My books are carried in all major libraries and bookstores.

Bliss List: I am serving humanity.

Measures of success:

1. I have influenced millions of people.

2. I have received thousands of testimonials from people sharing how I have improved their lives.

3. I am making the world a better place to live each day.

4. My books are carried in all major libraries and bookstores.

5. My messages have been quoted by others who are serving humanity.

Bliss List: I own a dream house on the ocean.

Measures of success:

1. The view from my patio is spectacular.

2. I hear seagulls every morning.

3. I see the sunrise over the water each morning.

4. My house is valued at over $2 million.

5. I enjoy swimming in the ocean and walking along the shore each day.

CREATE YOUR BLISS BOARD

"When you change the way you look at things,
the things you look at change."
Dr. Wayne Dyer

Let's start with your office. What do you look at? Let's start with your screen saver and walls. Do you have any goals or desires in plain view? The more intensity you give to your thoughts, the stronger they become. Your attention to your goals allows them to manifest more quickly in your life. A powerful tool to help you strengthen your thoughts and vibration and obtain your bliss more quickly is to use a Bliss Board.

As the name implies, a Bliss Board is basically a bulletin board. It is comprised of your goals and desires. Vivid, colorful pictures are ideal and very powerful. Fill your Bliss Board with words and phrases that describe what makes you happy. Whatever you desire and think about with enthusiasm and confidence will manifest itself.

You can have more than one Bliss Board. I keep at least three Bliss Boards in my office, along with framed affirmations such as these: "Money Comes Easily and Frequently," "Every Day, in Every Way, I am Getting Better, Better, and Better," "Negative Thoughts, Negative Suggestions, Have No Influence over Me at Any Level of Mind," and "Desire, Believe, Expect, and Be Grateful."

The trick is to keep your mind laser-focused on what you truly want. Meditating and visualizing your Bliss Boards and affirmations also magnifies your vibration tremendously. The more you can intensify your goals, the more likely it is that you will obtain them.

Be creative with your Bliss Board. Have fun with it. The more realistic you can make it—using pictures in 3D and colors that appeal to you—the more effective it will be. Cut out pictures from magazines or print colored images from the Internet. Place your Bliss Board in a prominent location where you will see it often.

I keep my three Bliss Boards at eye level right around my computer screen, and every time I look at them (and it is often), I always try to feel as though my goals and desires are in the present—as if I already have them.

What is on my three Bliss Boards? My first is a diagram of "Six Spokes of Bliss," with an individual listing of each one: Financial, Relational, Emotional, Intellectual, Physical, and Spiritual. More about this important concept in Chapter 3.

My second is my current Bliss List in text form which includes:

1. A financial goal for this year
2. A financial goal for the next three years
3. Specific speaking engagement targets
4. "Writing a New Book"

5. "Healthy, Loving Relationships with Everyone"
6. "Quality Time with Loved Ones"
7. "Help over 100,000,000 People"

My third contains pictures of:

1. My dream house
2. My dream car
3. Popular TV talk-show hosts/hostesses I'd love to meet in studio
4. My loved ones
5. The cover of my new book with a #1 Bestseller tag
6. A Barnes and Noble bestseller shelf with my books
7. An Amazon Top 100 sign

On all three of my Bliss Boards, I include the all-important tag at the end, "Or Something Better!" This sounds simple but is important to do each time. You may not be setting a high enough goal for yourself.

Though my first Bliss Board technically had six items rather than the recommended seven, don't get hung up about the numbers on your Bliss Board. The more you can add—without clutter—the better. Notice how I used pictures and words? Some say pictures are preferred, but most agree, a combination of pictures and words works wonders.

Since you are one of the 100,000,000 who bought this book and are actually reading it, I am one step closer to one of my goals. I am grateful for you.

Make a Bliss Board. It only takes a few minutes to do. You already have a *Top Seven Bliss List*, so it should be easy and fun. The results will amaze you.

FILL YOUR BLISS JAR

Take a jar (I use an empty green-olive jar from my favorite brand) and tape a note on top of the jar stating, "Whatever is contained in this Bliss Jar—IS!" Write each goal individually on a small piece of paper, then reread it with enthusiastic feeling, and simply drop each one into the jar. You will be amazed at how many of your little notes actually come true.

Now, write out your blissful dream job description on a piece of paper and reread it; then drop it into your jar.

Every single goal I have deposited into my Bliss Jar has miraculously come true. Bliss Jars make miracles seem common. It takes only a few minutes to write and drop your wishes into a jar, but the results will astound you—and may last a lifetime.

To get started, you may want to use the 15 items you listed in your original *Bliss List*. Though you pared the list down to seven so you wouldn't overload your brain (which is capable of handling only seven things at once), you cannot overload your Bliss Jar. There are no limits. Write all 15 goals down separately and drop them into the jar. It will start working its magic right after you close the lid.

The first time something you wrote comes true—and it will—start a new jar. Label it your "Gratitude Jar" and pop each item as it comes true into the new jar. This will serve as a constant reminder of your gratitude and the fact that your Bliss Jar works.

The more you can formalize your thoughts, the more likely your goals will manifest. Bliss Lists, Cards, Boards, and Jars all help bring your desires into reality.

In the next chapter, we will delve into pitfalls that can derail you from your bliss. As you improve your focus on what you truly want, while avoiding obstacles, you will find your bliss.

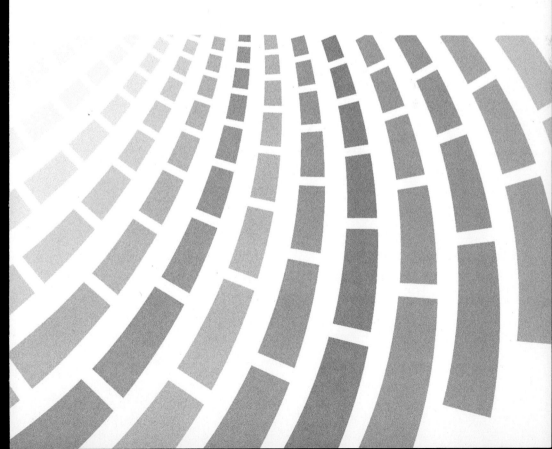

2

Four-Letter Words and Buckets

Change is eternal, progress divine.

From now on, four-letter words will no longer be allowed in your vocabulary. Four-letter words are seemingly everywhere: in our conversations, in books we read, at athletic events, in business circles, on radio, and certainly on TV. Four-letter words have become part of our psyche and are truly toxic.

You are probably thinking, "What's the big deal with saying or hearing *sh#t, f#%k* or *d&mn*?" I'm not referring to *those* words (though those words, commonly referred to as *swear words,* are probably not the most enlightened form of communication). I'm referring to the most damaging of four-letter words: *can't, don't,* and *won't.*

The human spirit is truly limitless. Look at all the things that have been invented over the years by mankind: electricity, automobiles, airplanes, a space ship to the moon, and numerous cures for a host of diseases. In every case, one common denominator pervades: a positive attitude and a can-do approach.

Henry Ford, the inventor of the automobile, said, "Whether you think you can or think you can't, either way you are right." Profound.

At the time he was chasing his dream—a motorized form of transportation—people ridiculed him, calling him crazy for having such a wild vision. His friends actually tried to have him locked up in an insane asylum! Amid all the criticism from some very intelligent people, Henry Ford kept his dream alive with a positive attitude, always saying and believing *I think I can.*

Had he fallen into the trap of the four-letter words, do you think he would have invented anything, let alone something as complex as a motorized car? Absolutely not. Any time you say or think *can't, don't,* and *won't,* you are placing limits on yourself.

Think about it in terms of natural resources. Your greatest natural resource is yourself. Almost everyone at some point has experienced physical exhaustion through exercise. When you work out vigorously, you probably use 60 to 90 percent of your body's potential. You know this through the outward sign of physical exertion—sweat. Sweat is your body's way of communicating that your physical movements in the form of exercise are working.

We work out to achieve desired goals: a better physique, losing weight, building muscle, for example. If you go into it with a positive attitude, chances are the exercise will be successful. I *can* run a mile in under eight minutes, I *can* lift one hundred pounds over my head, and I *can* ride my bike around the lake. After you achieve your goal, you feel good; if you fall short, you probably resolve to try harder next time and eventually achieve your goal. If a four-letter word enters your psyche, though, you will never make it.

While I was coaching my son's fifth-grade basketball team, we put this theory to the test with free throws. We had just lost a close game (that we should have won) because we didn't make our free throws at the end of the game. The other team did. Since we practiced the shot more than any other team, I was puzzled. My instincts told me the problem wasn't physical (lack of practice) but attitudinal.

I pulled my team together and explained the power of a positive attitude and its direct proportion to success: in this case, making the shot. Conversely, I discussed what happens when negative thoughts enter your mind before shooting. The boys looked aloof and somewhat puzzled, giving me that "can't we just play, coach?" look. I knew I was running out of time with a bunch of ten-year-olds, so we quickly put it to the test.

First, I had each boy mentally say, "Make the shot," and then shoot two free throws in a row; next, I had them shoot two more shots after mentally saying, "Don't miss." Remember, the subconscious mind doesn't discern between do and don't—it picks up the predominant thought—in this case, "miss."

The results were remarkable. The percentage of shots made with a positive thought versus a negative thought was over 50 percent. Those of you who understand basketball know that many games are decided by one point (a single free throw) and a 50 percent advantage was huge.

We further tested the theory with five shots and used the same positive and negative mantras. The results were even more compelling. The boys became believers in positive thinking, and we soon became the best free throw shooting team in the league. All it took was focusing their thoughts on a positive. Try this same exercise using any measuring stick. You don't need a basketball.

If you are like the average person, you will use less than 5 percent of your brain throughout your life. Drawing an analogy to our exercise example, you conversely use between 60 to 90 percent of your body while working out. Why the discrepancy? Is your physique that much more capable of working to its capacity than your mind?

You know the answer. Then why do you underutilize your mind? Do the four-letter words have anything to do with it? Of course, they do. You place limits on yourself any time you say, "I can't do this" or "I won't try this" or "It doesn't work." Henry Ford figured it out: "Whether you think you can or think you can't, either way you are right." Your words reflect your thoughts and become your results.

If you are going to get your blissful dream job, you have to commit to dropping the four-letter words from your vocabulary, your thoughts, and your actions. These toxic terms infect your psyche and limit you to using less than 5 percent of your greatest natural resource—your mind. A positive, can-do attitude is the difference between success and failure. It's that simple.

NO LIMITS

You are created as an unlimited spiritual being. The only limitations you have are in your mind, in the form of fear. What is fear? Fear is:

*F*alse

*E*vidence

*A*ppearing

*R*eal

If you hold the concept of limitation, it becomes reality, but the concept of limitation is not true. A hindrance (limitation) may appear real, but it is not. Four-letter words are a form of limitation. A toxic form. The great news is that all limitations can easily be released from you. They are *not you* to begin with.

You're probably saying, "Not me—I'd never let my mind become polluted!" I talk to people all the time who don't even realize they are doing it. I hear the following phrases/words often:

- *I'm not ever going to be rich.*
- *I'm not management material.*
- *I'm not smart enough.*
- *I'm fat because it's in my genes.*
- *I couldn't ever be like him/her.*
- *My father died at sixty-seven. I probably will too.*
- *There's no way I could ever match that.*

Have you ever said any of these? They are all limitations. Are they real? Sure, if you make them real by placing your attention on any of them. The upshot: by using another universal law, the Law of Polarity, you can discharge all toxic limitations. They were not you to begin with, so they can be released with a little conscious effort using your disciplined mind.

The Law of Polarity states simply that everything has a polar opposite. For every positive, there is a negative (think of a magnet here): yin/yang, plus/minus, dark/light. Do you ever wonder why, in a world of unlimited abundance, you sometimes go through events, conditions, and circumstances that you perceive as unpleasant? Becoming aware and developing a deeper understanding concerning the Law of Polarity may provide the insight that you need to obtain your bliss:

- *Can't* becomes *can.*
- *Don't* becomes *do.*
- *Won't* becomes *will.*
- *I'm never going to be rich* becomes *money comes easily and frequently.*
- *I'm never going to find love* becomes *all the love I'll ever need is already inside me.*

THE STORY OF PAUL

I have known Paul for over 25 years. We were friends at Boston College, he was in my wedding party, and to this day, even though we live a thousand miles away, he has remained one of my closest friends.

Paul is very bright. He graduated as *Scholar of the College* at Boston

College. While the rest of us were *partying like it was 1999* (in 1984), during our senior year, Paul was working hard at writing his mini-thesis, which later earned him his award.

After college, Paul attended Fordham Law School in New York near his hometown. He followed in his father's footsteps by attending law school. After excelling in law school, Paul passed the New York Bar Exam on his first try, and voilà, he was in his chosen profession. The only problem was that he hated it!

Paul changed firms a few times and even changed the types of law he practiced, but it didn't matter—he still hated it. Every time I talked to him, he was in a state of depression—complaining about the money not being what he wanted, the high cost of having an office in Manhattan, and even the work itself. Paul was certainly among the four out of five people unhappy in their jobs.

For someone to attend graduate school for a chosen profession (especially the brutal three years of law school) only to discover he hates it, the feeling of depression must have been devastating. It's a lot easier to quit that job flipping burgers at McDonald's (my first job) than to walk away from a profession that was dearly earned and outwardly admired.

So, let's take a step back and examine Paul's dilemma. You might be thinking the same thing I was whenever I would visit with him: "You are a successful attorney, making good money, working in Manhattan, living in Westchester, married to a beautiful doctor, with two gorgeous daughters. Paul, most people would trade places with you in an instant. What is the problem?"

The truth is all the externals didn't make his internal happy. He had zero passion for what he was doing. He was sinking in quicksand.

Rather than wallow in self-pity and ultimately self-destructing like so many others, Paul did something different. He changed his mindset and set some new goals. He developed a patent. He had an idea for a software enhancement, and he wrote it down. It was his "aha" moment. He felt tremendous joy because he knew it would be worth something someday.

Then, he did it again. He had another idea, and "BOOM," it turned into another patent. And then another. It was as if time stood still for Paul as he was doing this. His creative juices were flowing overtime, and he was rapidly becoming a patent expert.

While still going through the motions of being a lawyer, he used his spare time thinking about improving things in his daily life, and he wrote them down. He noticed the obvious: he was passionate about writing patents.

The next step was to see if his ideas had any value. He was blown away. His first patent was auctioned for six figures. The time it took him to have his idea was less than a minute and was now worth over $100,000. The second patent auction was also very lucrative. And so was the third. Paul was approached by a successful firm specializing in marketing patents and was asked to join them as a partner. He jumped at the offer.

Paul is like a new man—actually more like a little kid with a new toy. He is so upbeat, he's borderline giddy. Gone are his feelings of despair and depression. Long gone. In a short while, he has made a small fortune, but more importantly, he found his dream job. It doesn't feel like a job to him. He enjoys waking up and going to work. He is now part of a group that shares in the wealth of others' ideas.

While I was lounging with Paul poolside in Las Vegas, his cell phone rang. He found out he made another six figures—from someone else's efforts. Napoleon Hill (author of *Think and Grow Rich*) wrote about the power of joining forces with others with similar vision. Paul is now living proof of the wisdom of Napoleon Hill. On a personal note, Paul has lost weight, feels great, and is a man who is living the dream at work and beyond.

Let's take a minute to look at what happened to Paul. He became a lawyer with the strong influence of his father, who was a very successful attorney. Though Paul was successful in the profession of law, he was living someone else's dream—not his own. He gave it a shot, and when it wasn't what he wanted, he did the first thing needed to make a change. He attracted what he *did* want into his life. His ideas came to him with seemingly little effort. He set goals, had enthusiasm, and, as each idea materialized, his confidence grew.

A blissful dream job should feel like a *vacation,* not a *vocation.* Paul felt like he was on vacation. Time stood still for Paul. He followed his inner voice, his true passion, and it rewarded him. He knew he was meant to develop and market patents. To get there, though, Paul had the following:

- **Vision**. He focused his goals on what he wanted to do and the results followed.
- **Belief**. He believed in himself and in his ideas.
- **Positive attitude**. While he was developing his ideas, he became optimistic.
- **Awareness**. He was tuned in to signs along the way and acted on them.
- **Wisdom**. His ideas translated into successful practical applications.
- **Initiative**. He followed his inner push.
- **Discipline**. He made it a habit to create ideas.
- **Action**. He took the time to write down his ideas and apply them.
- **Inner success**. Though the money was great, his real triumph was inner joy for finding what he was passionate about and doing it.

On the other hand, a number of obstacles like these could have gotten in his way, derailing his dream job:

- *I don't have time* excuse. A toxic and limiting four-letter word. Less than a minute to make $100,000?

- *I can't do that* excuse. Four-letter word. He believed in himself.

- *I won't be able to sell this* excuse. Four-letter word. Defeatism.

- *My wife won't let me* excuse. Another four-letter word. Toxic.

- *My dad will think I'm nuts* excuse. In hindsight, your dad would think you were *nuts* for not doing this sooner. And if not, who cares. It's not his life or his dream job. Send him a copy of your bank statement, and he'll ask if he can join you.

- *I'll let my law partners down* excuse. Are they living your life? You are letting them down by being depressed about the very job you're trying to share with them. Misery never produced greatness unless it's expressed in a poem or a song.

- *My friends will think I'm crazy* excuse. Are they really your friends then? Your true friends want to see you happy first. If it means chasing your dream and they're not happy, well, it's definitely time for new friends. Mediocrity attacks excellence.

Get the picture? You may be saying, that's a great story, but I can't do that. Hopefully, by now, you will catch the four-letter word and reverse the toxic thought. I hope you said, "Hey! I could do that." And you could. And you will.

How many times have you seen something and said, "I could improve that?" It's what Paul did. It took him less than a minute for the idea to pop into his head. When it did, it felt right to him. He followed his sixth sense—his inner intuition. He acted on it and time stood still.

Now, I'm not saying your dream job needs to be Paul's, but it was easier for him to make that move than you think. And, aren't we all inventors? You see something that's broken and you fix it. No manuals needed. No graduate degree needed. You just do it. If you count the number of times you see something and think of a better way, you will amaze yourself. Paul acted on it. His confidence paid off.

First and foremost, Paul needed to develop a goal to break out of his doldrums, by saying, "I intend to find my bliss." Everyone can do that. Then, the more enthusiastically he desired it, the more his vision began manifesting itself. He was aware of signs along the way. He acted on those signs and persevered. His vocation became a vacation.

What is holding you back from obtaining your bliss? Everything is possible in your life.

Has anyone ever told you to do something because of money: "Be a doctor, you'll make lots of money"? Or in reverse, has anyone ever discouraged you with the threat of not making money: "There's not much money in that" or "Don't do that; you can't make any money doing that"? (Notice the four-letter words.) Did you ever receive advice like this? Did it sway you?

Plenty of doctors, lawyers, accountants, dentists, and executives earn good money but hate what they do. Paul is not the only example. How can this be? If money was their motivation, devoid of passion, are you surprised? There are many unhappy, wealthy people. I talk to them all day long in my executive search business.

External forces that cause you to stray from your inner wisdom need to be recognized and cancelled. Only your inner essence knows what is best for you.

POSITIVE PSYCHOLOGY 101

Wouldn't this be a cool class to take in school? It isn't listed on many college curriculums yet, but if it were, I would sign up in a heartbeat.

What is the field of psychology based on? Hint: it's the opposite of positive. Picture the shrink, inviting you to lie down on his or her couch and, with a slight frown, asking, "What brings you here?," which translates to most as *what's wrong?*

By now, you've had a big enough dose of the Law of Attraction, so where does thinking about what's wrong fit in your frame of reference? What will focusing on what's wrong attract back to you? The answers: more of what's wrong. This form of psychology is wrong!

Imagine what would happen if psychology began focusing on *what's right* with people? Asking, "What's wrong with you?" automatically pops you into a negative reference point. It makes you feel lousy as you think of the answer and then even worsens as you begin to verbalize your response. Asking "What's right?" places you in a positive emotional state and makes you feel good as you formulate your answer to the question.

It only takes seventeen seconds to change your emotional mood. If you feel depressed, in merely seventeen seconds, by changing your thoughts to joy, gratitude, love, or happiness, you leave that depression behind and start attracting desirable results. Increasing your positive emotions could lengthen your lifespan by ten years.

In the 1950s, psychology professor Don Clifton, PhD, began researching and pioneering positive psychology while teaching at the University of Nebraska. After conducting a significant number of interviews, Dr. Clifton wrote the fabulous book *How Full Is Your Bucket?* and later, as CEO of the Gallup Organization, began implementing positive psychology into one of the greatest corporate cultures in the world. In 2002, one year before his death, Dr. Clifton was recognized by the American Psychological Association as the "Grandfather of Positive Psychology."

Your life is really based on relationships, isn't it? You weren't placed here to live alone like a hermit; you were placed here to interact and build relationships throughout life. Dr. Clifton discovered that your life is defined by your relationships and how you interact with others. He viewed each interaction as having a profound effect on your psyche.

Your emotions are rarely neutral; they are either positive or negative (just like love and fear). The same holds true for your interactions; they, too, are almost always positive or negative. Though you may take these interactions for granted by living in default with an undisciplined mind, they have a cumulative effect on you. Dr. Clifton used a simple analogy involving a bucket and a dipper—very profound in its simplicity.

How does it work? In a nutshell, everyone has an invisible bucket. It is emptied or filled with each interaction, depending on what others say or do to you. When your "bucket" is filled up, you feel great; when it's empty, you feel lousy. Everyone has an invisible dipper. Whenever you use your dipper to say or do something to increase someone else's positive emotions, you fill their bucket, and your own, at the same time.

Conversely, by saying or doing something to cause negative emotions, you diminish that other person as well as yourself. This is a creative way to discipline your mind to direct the Law of Attraction to really work for you. Dr. Clifton inspired every employee at Gallup to institute this simple conscious philosophy into each interaction.

As a result, his employees developed disciplined minds. He took the age-old saying, "If you can't say something nice about someone else, don't say anything at all," and improved it to, "Say something nice always and nice will happen to you." The Law of Attraction, karma, and The Golden Rule in a new form: a bucket and a dipper.

During the Korean War, imprisonment in the North Korean POW camps resulted in a 38 percent death rate—the highest in U.S. military history. Yet, the prisoners weren't tortured; they were provided adequate food, water, and shelter. In fact, fewer cases of physical abuse were reported in the North Korean POW camps than in prison camps from any other major military conflict throughout history.

How can this be? Why did POWs die? Disease? On the contrary, the captives were provided adequate medical attention. No tsunami either. Run out of reasons? The North Koreans employed the most deadly form of torture—negativity.

After the Korean War, Major (Dr.) William Mayer—who would later become the U.S. Army's chief psychiatrist—studied over a thousand Americans detained as prisoners of war in a North Korean camp. Dr. Mayer discovered that the North Koreans' primary objective was to "deny men the emotional support that comes from interpersonal relationships." They systemically encouraged and rewarded prisoners who ratted out their fellow U.S. soldiers, criticized themselves, and broke loyalty to their leaders and their country.

All positive letters from home were destroyed; only news of negativity was passed along, such as a death in the family, spousal separation, and financial turmoil. In short, they broke the prisoners' spirits with constant negativity, causing them to completely give up mentally, physically, and emotionally. Dr. Clifton was so moved by Dr. Mayer's research that it inspired him to create positive psychology and put his theories into practice.

It stands to reason that by applying the Law of Polarity (everything has a polar opposite), the reverse results can happen with an environment of positives. This is exactly what Dr. Clifton was able to do with the Gallup Organization and through his book for those who implemented the bucket and dipper concept into their workplaces.

Earlier, you read that four out of five people are unhappy in their jobs and that we would examine the one out of five who is happy. Dr. Clifton proved that he could create a culture of happiness, using his bucket and dipper theory. By having employees keep a bucket on their desks and challenging them to consciously become "bucket fillers," he created a workplace where the majority—even more than one out of five—became happy in their jobs. Bucket fillers find bliss in their jobs. It's that simple.

Are you a bucket filler? Do you make others feel positive emotions with the majority of your words and actions? Your bliss is tied to this basic tenet of positive psychology. Practice positive psychology yourself and you will find your bliss.

ARE YOU LIVING THE DREAM AND SAYING SO?

Whenever someone asks me how I'm doing, I love to enthusiastically answer, "Living the dream." People will look at me funny, half wondering if I am for real or just plain nuts (in my case, both are true).

I can tell a lot about people and where they are in their lives after asking the simple question, "How are you doing?" If the answer is, "Not bad," uh oh, that translates to *bad*. "Can't complain" means *complaining*. "All things considered, I'm okay." Just okay? Not many great things have ever been accomplished with *just okay* ambitions.

How do you answer the question, "How are you doing?" Do you answer, "Not bad," "Can't complain," or "Okay?" Try answering, "Living the dream" and see if the other person looks at you as if you're crazy. Know what's crazy? Actually thinking and, in turn, believing, you are "not bad," or "can't complain," or just "okay."

The point is this: words have tremendous meaning. Your words are actually energy. They are the building block in your energy hierarchy; it starts with your words, then your thoughts, and culminates with your emotions. Your emotions are guided by your words and then your thoughts. So your emotions are your highest form of energy emitted in the form of a vibration. Think of your emotion as energy in motion.

The more negative you are in your words—as we discussed with four-letter words—the more negative results you will attract. The great news is that your words can also attract what you really want. From now on, answer the question, "How are you doing?" with "Fantastic!" "Great!" "Living the dream!" or "Outstanding!" And mean it.

So many people actually deflate their self image with their own words. At some point, you've probably said, "I'm so stupid" or "I'm such an idiot" or "I'm so clumsy"—you get the point. You rarely hear someone say, "I'm great!"

My challenge to you is to apply positive psychology through your positive words. Remember, the more disciplined your mind, the greater your results. Your subconscious cannot discriminate what you say (between *don't* versus *do*), so think before you speak. And make positive affirmations your way of life—your automatic thought.

- "I can't wait for . . ." only pushes what you say further away from you. Say, "I'm excited for . . ."
- "I feel lousy" will only make you feel worse. Say, "I feel healthy" and you will start attracting good health.
- "I'm sick" will only worsen your condition. Say, "I'm grateful to feel vibrant and healthy." (Obviously, in front of your doctor, articulate your symptoms, but then say "Cancel" to yourself and don't dwell on suffering.)
- "I don't want to be broke" will bankrupt you eventually (I hear this one a lot). Say, "I wish to be financially independent and abundantly prosperous."
- "I hate this job" becomes, "I'm grateful for the contrast I've learned in this job. I now know what I desire in my next job."

- "I hate my boss" becomes, "I'm grateful for the contrast I've learned from my boss. I now know the type of boss I truly desire and deserve."
- "Life stinks" becomes, "Life's full of bliss."

WORDS MAKE WATER SMILE

Dr. Masaru Emoto examined the effect words have on water. In his book *The Hidden Messages in Water,* Dr. Emoto proved with factual evidence that human vibrational energy, thoughts, words, ideas, and music affect the molecular structure of water. Through high-powered photography, Dr. Emoto published pictures of what water looked like after saying, "Thank you," "Love and appreciation," "Soul," "Love plus gratitude," and "Mother Teresa." The result was amazing: the water was transformed from ordinary form into beautiful crystals.

The polar opposite also held true. Words like "You make me sick—I will kill you," "Adolf Hitler," and "Hate" transformed the water into nasty images. Even polluted, filthy looking water could be transformed into beautiful shapes with positive words. See an analogy here? Mind pollution can be cleared up with the right goals (words that stem from thoughts) which, with enthusiasm and confidence, become you.

Water comprises over 70 percent of a human body and, for that matter, covers the same amount of our planet. Water is the very source of all life on this planet. Its quality and integrity are vitally important to all forms of life. Your body is very much like a sponge and is composed of trillions of chambers called "cells," which hold liquid. The quality of your life is directly connected to the quality of your water. What are toxic words doing to your "body" of water?

You get the picture. I hope this doesn't seem trivial and trite to you because the Law of Attraction is what you make of it. You hold the building blocks, and the area in which you may build is limitless. Take control of your words, thoughts, and feelings and then your results will resemble beautiful crystals. Every time.

When someone asks you, "How are you doing?" answer "Living the dream!" You may even make them smile—and turn your water into beautiful crystals.

WHAT'S YOUR PASSION (AND IT'S NOT ABOUT THE MONEY)

"If you always do what interests you,
at least one person will be pleased."
Katharine Hepburn

I recently spoke with Eric, a wealthy surgeon who was miserable. He didn't like his job. When I asked why he stayed with it, his answer was, "It pays the bills!" That wasn't an answer to my question, so I asked again, "Why don't you like your job?"

"The hours are brutal and malpractice insurance is outrageous!" he bemoaned.

I persisted, "Well, what would be your dream job?"

"Huh?"

"What job would make you happy?"

"Well, one with a lot fewer hours."

"Don't you control your own schedule?"

"Yes and no," he said.

"What do you mean?"

"I don't schedule surgeries or appointments."

"Who does?"

"Admin people."

"How many hours do you work in a given day?" I asked him.

"All day long!"

"Describe a typical day?"

"I'm here by 8:30 every day."

"Do you see patients then?"

"My first appointment is usually at 9 AM and my last is done by 6 PM."

"Do you take lunch or any breaks?" I wanted to know.

"I usually skip lunch or eat on the fly between appointments—and FORGET about breaks."

"How many days are you in surgery?"

"Two."

"Weekends?"

"No, thank God. But I bring tons of work home with me."

"What kind of work?"

"Paperwork, x-rays, files."

"When do you have time for your lovely wife?"

"Never. We hardly see each other and when we do, we usually fight, or she just nags me," he said.

Let's examine this scenario for a moment. Here's a guy driving a black Porsche (dream car), living in a mansion overlooking a beautiful, private golf course (dream house), making big bucks with a very attractive wife (dream spouse) and three great kids (dream family). He's brilliant. On the surface, he has it all. And yet, he is bankrupt inside. Why is he miserable in his job? Well, it's not about the money. And his misery in his job infects his relationship with his spouse, his kids, and, most importantly, with himself.

He was feeling drained and stressed out to the max. He looked ten years older than he was, complete with bags under his eyes, as he sat there moaning. He was having his own pity party right in front of me. By now, you know my advice (it's tough to feel any pity for a man with so many obvious blessings). But his problems were real—to him. His problems were all attitudinal and his attitude stunk! He was allowing his schedule to drain him further. In fact, he could control his own schedule if he truly wanted to.

Obviously, it wasn't really the schedule (8:30–6, Monday to Friday). It was his attitude. He was rationalizing his business. Said another way, he was *RATION-LIES-ing* his *BUSY-NESS*. He felt overworked, therefore, he was overworked. He blamed others when there really was only one place for any blame—inside. His glass was empty. He was caging himself in. And, ironically, he had the keys to unlock his own cage and to re-discover his own freedom. It started with gratitude, which was completely missing in his psyche.

A dream job is a relational experience—knowing you are doing something that makes the world a better place. There are three primary forms of relationships: (1) self, (2) others, and (3) environment. My friend was zero for three. He wasn't taking care of himself physically, mentally, or emotionally. He did not love himself.

This lack of love of self carried over into relationships with others; he was constantly complaining and miserable to be around. His relationship with environment was a failure also. He couldn't see beauty in anything. He complained that his house wasn't enough and that he was sick of the weather and he wasn't making enough money. He was a taker, not a giver; a victim, not a grateful professional living in financially abundant prosperity.

I asked him why he chose to become a doctor. He said, "My dad was a doctor and he always made good money so I just figured since I had good enough grades, I could become a doctor too."

Time for an assessment of my friend the miserable doctor:

- The motivation for his job was based on heredity and not on what he was passionate about (chances are his father wasn't happy either). His father always said to him, "I want you to become a doctor," but my friend never truly said, "I want to become a doctor." When others make your decisions, don't be surprised when they backfire.

- Money was the driving force behind his job choice. He is not alone; most people in professional jobs list money as one of the top reasons for choosing their particular profession. Yet, why are so many professionals—doctors, lawyers, accountants, dentists, and executives—unhappy? After all, they rank money number one, and they make plenty of the green stuff. Money alone is clearly not their workplace joystick.

You are a spiritual being living in a physical world. Your essence, your real driving force as a spiritual being, is in your three primary relationships: self, others, and environment. This means feeling appreciated by others and appreciating your own self and the world around you. Your true inner core is love, joy, wisdom, and abundance. If you cling to a material possession like money on a cosmic level, that alone cannot bring true happiness.

Ever visit someone on their death bed? They never say, "Oh, if only I made another hundred grand." Rather, they say, "Tell so and so I love them." It's about relationships. Mother Teresa said it well: "Even the rich are hungry for love, for being cared for, for being wanted, for having someone to call their own."

There is another reason why money alone doesn't bring happiness. Often, the focus is on scarcity—on lack of money. The negative thought, "I don't have enough money"—even if you are bringing in six or even seven figures—actually causes you to never have enough of that green stuff. And, after a while, this becomes a pattern (paradigm) that perpetuates itself. Unless the focus is on abundance and financial independence, your energies are focused on scarcity. The Universe responds to your vibration with poof: scarcity city!

Passion means finding the vocation that feels like a vacation— the point when time does stand still for you—when you are in a zone. And here's the rub: only you know your blissful dream job. Your parents, teachers, clergy, buddies, or spouse—even though they may seem to know you, they don't know. You now understand that external forces only pull you away from your inner self if you are not careful.

THE GEEKS HAVE THE LAST LAUGH

Some of the most interesting and important people throughout time were considered outcasts—today we'd refer to them as "geeks." Aristotle, Jesus, Gandhi, Shakespeare, Galileo, Einstein, Beethoven, Abe Lincoln, and Henry Ford, to name a few, were considered by "proper society" to be outcasts. Many of them were even brutally killed for their beliefs.

Their common trait? An unyielding inner strength and total confidence in what they believed in. Whether it was composing music, leading people to freedom, dying for the forgiveness of mankind's sins, building a car, or visualizing a new scientific discovery, all these people were true to their inner voice—their passion.

When we are connected with our inner wisdom, we are in our dream job state. Even if others call you a geek, it doesn't matter. If someone is trying to disconnect you from your inner harmony, then he or she is worse than a geek.

Remember, mediocrity attacks excellence, and if you are going to pursue your dreams, your social life may change. Friends will likely question you and may even belittle you for your desired aspirations. Henry Ford's "friends" tried to have him committed to a mental institution because of his passion for building the first commercial automobile. Where do you think Ford's friends were: in challenge mode or sitting idle?

I'm glad Ford had the courage to ignore his so-called friends. Are your friends likely to want you to stay idle with them? Don't be surprised. As you rise to a higher plane in life, you will need to leave behind friends and peers who try to hold you back—even if they are well-meaning, but don't have ambition themselves. Bosses, friends, coworkers, family, and peers may not handle your quest for the new you (complete with lofty dreams) very well. You will learn that if they do not support you, then they're not friends, but foes. Good riddance.

There is a simple yet powerful phrase that French psychologist Dr. Emile Coué developed and integrated into his patients' psyche during hypnosis with thousands of documented cures for a variety of ailments: "Negative thoughts, negative suggestions, have no influence over me at any level of mind."

A very powerful statement when committed to your subconscious. If you don't allow mean-spirited criticism to infect the "new you," it won't.

Another phrase Dr. Coué is best known for, and also used to help heal thousands of documented patients, was this one: "Every day, in every way, I am getting better, better, and better."

This is equally powerful when committed into the subconscious under hypnosis. The good news: you don't need a hypnotist to benefit from these powerful phrases. Instead, you can use a technique I explain in the next section.

Fortunately, Aristotle, Jesus, Gandhi, Mother Teresa, Galileo, Shakespeare, Lincoln, Emerson, and Ford were unswayed from their bliss by others. When mediocrity (in other words, unfocused on the right things) attacks excellence (the new you) say, "Thank you *forgiving* me the experience," (pun intended!). Don't let the new you succumb to outside forces and pressures.

HOW TO SOLVE A PROBLEM WITH NO EFFORT

What if I told you solving problems is so easy that you could do it in your sleep? Would you try it? Sure you would.

By now, you know how powerful your subconscious mind is. You can tap into the infinite wisdom you already possess inside of you and harness it to solve your problems—in your sleep. Literally. That's right, you can use your dreams to help you solve a problem. With a little practice in "programming your dreams," you can become quite proficient. You will be amazed at how powerful this tool can be.

It's simple. Just do this: right before you fall asleep for the night, say to yourself, "I desire to have a dream that will contain information to solve (state your problem)."

Then, after stating the problem, say to yourself, "I will have such a dream, remember it, and understand it." Just as before, feel as if the problem is already solved—with confidence. Feel the gratitude you will experience for receiving the solution through your dream as if it has already happened. This is important.

Enhance the likelihood for success in controlling your dreams by meditation. While in the alpha state (a deep phase of meditation when your brain waves slow down), visualize the problem and mentally say, "I want to remember a dream of importance. I will remember a dream." Ideally, meditate just before you sleep.

After you "program" your dream, all you have to do is fall asleep. When you awaken—either in the middle of the night or in the morning, and before you do anything (you will likely still be in the alpha state of consciousness—the best way to retrieve the dream), write down everything you remember from your most vivid dream (keep a notepad and pen bedside).

Afterwards, search your notes for meaning. With patience and total belief, it will work. It may take a few nights before you start remembering your dreams. Stick with it. You will be amazed by what your dreams will tell you. The only caution is to search for answers for something important. Trivial problems usually get trivial answers.

At this point, you may be skeptical and even start calling me names. Well, I'll be okay: negative thoughts, and suggestions, have no influence over me at any level of mind. What if I could give you an example of a famous product that was "invented" through a dream? How about the sewing machine?

Elias Howe was trying to invent a machine that could sew clothing. Sewing by hand was tedious, time-consuming, and expensive. He knew there was a way, but was completely stumped and was racking his brain. He had a burning desire to solve this problem—he knew there had to be a method, but his mind was stuck. Then, he had a vivid dream—and remembered it: *A man was in a jungle surrounded by savages. They were coming menacingly close to him, their spears rising, then descending. Each spear had a hole in the tip.*

When Howe awakened, he knew this dream solved his burning question to the problem and, voilà, he designed the sewing machine.

Earlier, he could make the needle rise and descend, but not sew—until his dream told him to put the hole at the tip.

Quite a bit has been written about dream interpretation. Sigmund Freud was a pioneer in the subject. But don't get Freud's work confused with our application. Freud's patients did not program their dreams; they just had dreams and remembered them.

One of your greatest challenges is to have a disciplined mind, not an undisciplined mind. You are deliberately programming your dreams for a specific purpose, not just dreaming in default. Big difference. See a parallel with the development of your (conscious) mind? Programming your time (having a disciplined, focused mind) is also how you succeed while you are awake.

If Howe had not deliberately programmed his dream, we would not have the sewing machine. Back to Siggy. Imagine how Freud would have interpreted Howe's dream? (I couldn't pass that one up.)

If you can program yourself into a disciplined mind 24/7 (while sleeping and awake), imagine what you are capable of accomplishing! If you are struggling with "what's my true dream job?" try programming your dreams for an answer.

While writing this book, many times I awakened in the middle of a deep sleep and wrote until dawn. Most people would rather stick pins and needles in their eyes than do this at three o'clock in the morning, but I was in my *bliss zone.* Do you think it was a coincidence that I programmed my dream before falling asleep?

I use dream programming all the time in my search business. Recently, a new client hired me to find a VP of Sales for them. Their headquarters was in a city that wasn't exactly in the top ten most desirable cities—even in their eyes. They were resigned to the fact that they would have a tough time getting someone to move to their undesirable location. My database didn't turn up anybody in the general area of their headquarters on the first try, so rather than panic, that night I programmed a dream to give me clear guidance of where to look.

When I awakened the next morning, my first thought was to call a guy I had known for years—let's call him Matt. I hadn't spoken to Matt for a few months, but for some reason, I knew I had to call him that morning, and, at first, I was worried that he might be in trouble.

When I called Matt, he answered on the first ring. He said, "It's funny you called—I was just thinking of calling you" (I could hear the theme from the *Twilight Zone*). In the past, Matt would never consider relocating out of the Northeast. On this particular day, as Matt told me he was open to relocating to the Southeast (where the position was), I was stunned—was this the same guy?

I said, "I have a great opportunity there right now." Just after I told him the name of the city, Matt interrupted me and said, "You know my oldest son is going there on a baseball scholarship?"

With tingling up and down my spine, I blurted out, "Oh yeah . . . that's right." As he Google-mapped the headquarters address, he discovered the company was only one mile from the campus.

Still think it was a coincidence? There are no coincidences. The job was exactly what Matt was looking for—his dream job. I sent him in on the first interview. The client absolutely loved him! I placed him in the job with ease, and he is eternally grateful that I called him with the opportunity. He had no idea how easy it was to think of him—I followed my dream "hunch." I later called Matt and explained what had happened, and he now understands and practices the Law of Attraction. Now, he programs his dreams too.

Start tonight. Instead of wishing someone sweet dreams, how about wishing that person to have productive dreams.

YOU CONTROL YOUR BLISS

"The weak have remedies, the wise have joys;
superior wisdom is superior bliss."
Edward Young

I have thrown a lot of information at you, and I'm sure your head is spinning a little. If so, this is good. Challenge begets growth. As you have developed your *Bliss List*, you have gained superior wisdom. There was no point in jumping to the résumé section before you created your *Bliss List*, established your positive attitude, and dreamed about your dream job.

Any goal you set with enthusiastic confidence, becomes reality. The key to attracting your bliss lies in understanding and applying the amazing universal Law of Attraction. In order to attract your blissful dream job, you have to raise your energy (vibration) and be disciplined enough to keep it raised. You guide your thoughts and emotions. You reach for a feeling. Your spirit (subconscious) has domain over your mind, which has domain over your body. You can reach your spirit through meditation, programming your dreams, and by purifying your thoughts with positive emotion and matching, effective language.

There are plenty of helpful gimmicks to use to help you obtain your bliss, and I have given you some of them: Bliss Lists, Bliss Jars, Bliss Boards, Bliss Cards, for example. Beyond these helpful techniques, the essence of your bliss is you: "remembering" your inner spirit. The real trick is for you to turbo-charge your energy toward obtaining your goals with enthusiastic confidence and gratitude. You choose your emotional state; you choose how you allocate your time. And you have your blissful dream job already inside you. Your challenge is to remember it.

I am often asked, "How can I attract my blissful dream job?" The following is a recap of several suggestions, some mentioned earlier, with a few new ones to keep it fresh.

- Gratitude. Gratitude. Gratitude. The glass is not half full or half empty; it's always full—especially if you apply gratitude to everything. Start your day with gratitude and continue your day with gratitude. Develop an attitude of gratitude.

- Meditation. Meditate three times a day for 15 minutes per session (see the box nearby; I give you a simple way to meditate).

- Music. Listen to Beethoven's *Pastorale.* You saw what it did to water in Emoto's work.

- Exercise. Your body produces natural drugs that make you feel "high"—and they're free and legal.

- Seminars. Make the time to recharge your batteries; travel to an interesting place—it's well worth it.

- Attend religious services. Just entering into a place of worship will usually lift your spirits. Find the ones that inspire you (not make you feel guilty) and spend an hour.

- Be happy. Think about what makes you happy, and remember it when you are not.

- Comedy. Laughter from movies or "live" comedy are great ways to get in a good mood.

- Read a book that inspires you. Reread the ones that have most inspired you. It's like riding a bike; the more you read and reread (practice), the more automatic the message will become. I list the most profound books that have influenced me in a section at the back of this book called Read More, if you'd like some suggestions.

- Get a massage. Go to a spa.
- Dance. Sing. Sing and dance.
- Do yoga.
- Go for a scenic bike ride.
- Hike in the mountains. Go for a walk. Drive a scenic route.
- Sit on a park bench and listen to the birds singing and the children laughing.
- Pray.
- Hold a puppy or a kitten.
- Rest. Never underestimate the power of a power nap.
- Think about your goals—hang them on your wall, put them in your wallet/purse, in a jar, and in your mind. It all works. Visualize your dream job.
- Watch the *Planet Earth* DVD in surround sound.
- Keep yourself in a positive emotional state: first, for five minutes, then for a half hour, then an hour, and then all day long. Feel gratitude, joy, love, passion, enthusiasm, happiness, optimism, hope, wisdom, contentment, and peace throughout the day.
- Get in "The Now," that place where you are truly present, where guilt (past) and fear (future) cannot exist.
- Take deep breaths using your stomach. Inhale through your nose and exhale through your mouth.
- Watch the sun rise. Watch the sun set (notice how they both look different each time).
- Tell someone, "I love you"—and mean it.
- Have wild passionate lovemaking (wanted to see if you were still paying attention!).
- Relive your happiest childhood memory in your mind.

- Attend the symphony. Listen to the majestic beauty. Then close your eyes and get to the alpha level—and listen to the difference.
- Say hello to perfect strangers. When you say hello, smile. You use a lot fewer muscles to smile than to frown.
- Hold the door open for a perfect stranger.

HOW TO MEDITATE

For those of you who still find the term "meditate" hokey, insert "prayer" or even "deep thought." Rather than get caught up in terminology, I really want you to try it. For the "don't have time" boo birds (notice the four-letter word?), 15 minutes of simple meditation is the equivalent of two hours of sleep. There, I just saved you an hour and forty-five minutes, so what do you have to lose? Nothing. Just try it with an open (and relaxed) mind. Meditation is one of the many tools to use in obtaining your dream job.

I would not have been able to write this book without the magic of meditation.

Though it may be easier to lie down, it's not necessary. All you need to do is close your eyes, turn your gaze upward at about 20 degrees and focus on your breathing.

Breathe using your stomach and not your chest. Take deep, slow breaths. Just focus on your inhaling and exhaling. Keep focusing on your breathing; don't allow your mind to drift off.

If you find yourself thinking about something else,

recognize it but don't engage. Just say, "cancel," and bring yourself back to focusing on your breathing. With a little practice, this form of meditation will become easy for you and can be used anywhere.

Most of us are too busy to set aside time to meditate. You can put mindful meditation into your day. Here are some suggestions:

- Pay attention to your breathing or your environment when you stop at red lights.

- Before you go to sleep, and when you awaken, take some "mindful" breaths.

- Instead of allowing your mind to wander over the day's concerns, direct your attention to your breathing.

- Find a task that you do impatiently or unconsciously (standing in line or brushing your teeth, for example) and concentrate on the experience.

Make something that occurs several times during a day, such as answering the phone or buckling your seatbelt, a reminder to return to the present—that is, think about what you're doing and observe yourself doing it.

Can you think of any people who have blissful dream jobs? There are plenty of famous people who have said they love their jobs—who are in the *Bliss Zone*: Oprah Winfrey, Warren Buffett, Jimmy

Buffett, Henry Ford, Thomas Edison, Albert Einstein, Beethoven, William Shakespeare, John Grisham, Jose Silva, Bill Gates, Dr. Wayne Dyer, Michael Jordan, Doug Flutie, Steven Spielberg, Walt Disney, Katharine Hepburn, Jack Canfield, James Taylor, and Ronald Reagan, to name a few.

Each of these people is known for exuding confidence and being positive thinkers. Each has transcended his or her dreams into blissful dream jobs.

Finding bliss in a dream job is not limited to celebrity—it's also the guy who loves to wait on tables and makes your meal entertaining with his energy; it's the Disney tour guide who exudes joy in describing the place; it's the artist sitting in front of a scene, entranced with capturing the view on canvas. All these people have found their bliss and are *living the dream*. You can too. If you are not, I hope this section helped you understand why not; most importantly, you now know *you* control everything in your life— with your disciplined mind.

One of my best examples of someone in a dream job is my mother. She was the perfect 1950s housewife. My dad was the successful lawyer—the bread winner; my mom, the housewife. She raised four kids (raising me was like raising five), cooked every dinner like a chef, and ran an immaculate house (not an easy task with my two sisters). Think *Leave It to Beaver*: my mother was June Cleaver.

She accepted her "lot in life" gracefully, but I could tell doing the mundane homemaker duties wasn't her dream job. She was a voracious reader (the apple doesn't fall far from the tree); she loved volunteering for public television; she loved entertaining and laughing; and she even loved being a Den Mother for Cub Scouts. Her *Bliss List* probably wouldn't have had "changing diapers," "slaving over a stove," or "driving four kids all over town for sports/

activities." But she accepted her role. After we kids started moving out to college, things changed for my mother.

As the empty-nester phase was nearing, my mother developed her dream job. She and another "former housewife" and friend partnered in forming a company, which they named *Color & You*. They each worked out of their own homes and became clothing consultants. They used some scientific research (you look your best in the colors of one of the four "seasons"—such as winter, spring, summer, or fall) and marketed their ability to determine what looked best on their clients, plus they sold their own hypoallergenic, high-quality, makeup line.

The book *Dress for Success* had been a bestseller, so people were interested in looking their best for interviews and at work. My mother saw an opportunity and took action. *Color & You* was successful and became her dream job.

So if you are a homemaker or stay-at-home mom and perhaps feeling trapped in life, after reading this book, I hope this story inspires you to follow your intuitive dreams. A blissful dream job can—and does—happen later in life. My mother's story was early inspiration for me to write this book. (In case you're wondering, I'm a summer, body type "C." I look my best in solid, pastel, blue-based colors.)

The purpose of this section is to awaken you. In the beginning, I said that you control your bliss. By now, you are convinced—and it is incredibly empowering to know that you control your destiny. I hope you are now using all the helpful tricks and exercises discussed, but ultimately, it is you and only you who knows what's best for you—your blissful dream job.

The purpose of this more spiritual side or mystical third of this book was also to prepare you for the practical action phase next. As you worked through the material, you may have had some negative thoughts that might have hindered you, causing angst in your life and in your work. Being able to guide your thoughts and align your subconscious with your conscious mind is the key to obtaining your dream job.

Positive thoughts with positive emotions bring positive results.

The next chapter will bring those positive results into inner harmony.

3

The Six Spokes of Bliss

✳

There is no way to bliss; bliss is the way.

Imagine experiencing bliss all the time. When asked, "How are you doing?", by now, you know I answer: "Living the dream!" I love watching how people respond. They often ask, "How can I live the dream too?"

It's simple. Strengthen your Six Spokes of Bliss. I use this diagram as a header atop all three of my own Bliss Boards and in my executive life coaching. It works!

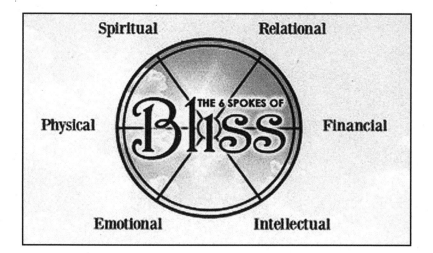

The Six Spokes of Bliss is a powerful guide to use to create a life of your dreams. Think of yourself as a wheel with six spokes: Financial, Intellectual, Emotional, Physical, Spiritual, and Relational. Notice they are all given the same importance. To work at your optimum level, each spoke needs to be as strong as possible. I want you to go six for six. You know what happens to a wheel with broken or rusty spokes? It may move but not very well. Go easy on yourself if a couple of your spokes are in need of repair.

We all know someone who may possess one spoke that is out of sync. For example, in the financial spoke—one of the most popular with my life coach clients—there are plenty of billionaires who are spiritually, physically, relationally, intellectually, and emotionally bankrupt (I'm not naming names, since they can afford better lawyers than me).

Scientists know that in only 21 days you can change any habit. I know many of you struggle just to know what you want. Developing goals for each spoke is the key to obtaining bliss. This chapter will help you get started, but it's up to you. Are you ready to make your own quantum leap into bliss?

Let's start by assessing each spoke. I'll ask you some basic questions. Take out a piece of paper or use your Bliss List Journal.

Financial

- What is your actual income?
- How much money will it take to obtain financial freedom? (Mortgage, car, credit card debt, etc.)
- What is your dream net worth?
- Rank yourself on a scale of 1–10 (ten being the highest, representing how close you think you are to where you want to be).

Intellectual

- How often do you read in an average day?
- How often do you write?
- How many seminars do you attend in a given year?
- How much time do you spend watching TV? (Be honest.)
- Rank yourself on a scale of 1–10.

Emotional

- Do you get enough sleep?
- Does the music you listen to relax you?
- How do you handle stress?
- Are you an optimist or a pessimist?
- Rank yourself on a scale of 1–10.

Physical

- Do you exercise a minimum of twenty minutes every day?
- Do you eat a healthy, nutrient rich diet?
- Are you at your ideal weight?
- Do you smoke, drink alcohol in excess, and/or use drugs?
- Rank yourself on a scale of 1–10.

Spiritual

- Do you have a strong connection with your creative source?
- Do you meditate each day?

- Do you pray each day?
- What makes time stand still for you? How often does it happen during an average day?
- Rank yourself on a scale of 1–10.

Relational

- Do you spend quality time alone?
- Do you treat yourself the way you want others to treat you?
- Describe your dream mate?
- If you have a dream mate already, do you spend quality time together?
- Are there people you hold grudges against?
- Do you have any enemies?
- Rank yourself on a scale of 1–10.

Did you learn anything about yourself while doing this exercise? I hope so. Did you score a perfect 60? If so, you might have passed away and are floating above this book. Have someone pinch you immediately. If you can feel it, give this book to someone else. If you scored a zero, go back and be easier on yourself. If you were truly honest, your score was somewhere in the middle; each spoke could use some strengthening. And, your score is always evolving. It's easy to let some spokes slide, but know that whatever you focus on will improve.

I'm going to give you a real-life example. I was flying home from my first national TV interview. I was behind about 12 hours of REM sleep, but a professional young lady sat next to me. We'll call her Wendy. She asked, "How are you doing?" You know my answer. She looked intrigued and just as she was going to comment, I asked, "How are you doing?" She replied, "Well, if I had more money, I'd be doing better." I sighed.

This is one of the most common complaints I hear as a life coach and executive search consultant. I knew my "Relaxation" folder on my iPod could wait.

I still had an extra book left over from my TV interview. Wendy spotted it and asked to see it. When she noticed my mug shot on the back cover, her level of excitement rose. She asked if I could give her some free life coaching.

Normally, I'd reply, "Something for nothing has no value." She seemed so enthused that I made an exception. I said, "Tell me about yourself." For the next hour, I listened to her complain about every aspect of her life: she was broke, despised her boss, felt under-utilized in her job, had relational problems, and felt overweight. Basically, she was zero for six.

I first explained that what she just described wasn't her at her core. That was who she used to be. I opened the book to the diagram of the Six Spokes of Bliss and mentioned the analogy to the wheel. Her eyes flashed interest. Next, I took out a piece of paper and asked her to set goals for what she wanted out of work and life—with an eye on each spoke. As she wrote, her mood shifted from despondent to enthusiastic. It was like flipping a switch. When she finished, she said she felt great about it.

I felt great about it too.

The plane began its descent, and Wendy said, "Can I buy your book?" I laughed and said, "You just told me how broke you were. The last thing I'm going to do is charge you 20 bucks you don't have. . . . Here, take it."

Her eyes sparkled, but she said, "No, I have to pay you. It's the least I can do for all your help." After a few back and forth's, the plane was nearing the runway. I said, "Okay, here's your charge: if you like the book, tell ten friends; if not, don't tell anyone."

Wendy giggled, then with piercing eyes, said, "I will."

After she left, I hoped she would commit to strengthening her spokes, but you never know. Helping her raised my spirits; I wasn't tired anymore.

Forty days later, I received an e-mail from Wendy through my website www.BlissList.com (yes, I actually read them). Her excitement nearly burst through my computer screen. Wendy had gone six for six on her goals! She had been promoted to director level, had a new boss who she loved, was making more money and saving (for a change), she lost weight, she was praying with more meaning, and her relationships were greatly improved. She wrote: "I ordered ten copies of the book and am giving them as Christmas presents to friends and family" (many of the very people she had admitted she was at odds with during our flight).

Then came the kicker. Now, as a director, she had the ability to purchase books for the entire company. She ordered a sizable number of copies of my book (my largest single sale to date!). Later, she hired me for two professional life coaching assignments and set me up to speak at the company's national meeting.

My encounter with Wendy reinforced one of my core beliefs: the more you give—without expecting anything in return—the greater your reward. Wendy helped change my previous paradigm—*something for nothing has no value*—to *life is for-giving* (pun intended). I'd say giving my time and book for free, with no expected return, paid enormous dividends!

Wendy's quantum leap stemmed from a conscious choice—to commit to strengthen her spokes. The result? In only 40 days, well ahead of her own deadline of six months, she was a whole new (and improved) person.

Are you ready to take the first step toward living the dream? Ready to determine what makes your vocation feel like a vacation—what makes time stand still for you?

Let's dive into each spoke and plant some action steps in you:

Financial: I'm going to devote the most ink to this spoke since everyone seems to struggle with this one. And they shouldn't. Consider this: when you pass away, does your financial spoke matter? (Not to you, but perhaps to others hoping to hit a jackpot off your will.) In time, money won't matter to them either, so let's allay the fears on money right now.

One of my executive life coaching clients earns over $350,000 per year yet feels poor. Huh? She is not alone. In *The Chaos Point*, author Ervin Laszlo wrote that 64 percent of Americans with an average wealth of $38 million or more still feel financially insecure! It's no wonder people struggle with this spoke. Believe it or not, the financial spoke is one of the easiest to master; once you know how. You control it.

What is money anyway? Think of it as energy. The entire universe is energy—your desk, computer, cell phone, this book, you. Energy is constantly moving in either particles or waves. Money—metal or paper—is energy also. Under a high-powered microscope, it's moving in particles and evolving. I want you to consider this to demystify the green stuff. You don't really own money; you are leasing it and serving as a conduit: you earn, you spend. It's that simple. See the green stuff as a transferring of energy.

Scientists know that money accounts for only ten percent of your happiness. So what makes you happy? Your attitude, including your attitude toward money. Too many people have an attitude of scarcity about money. See the glass as half-empty and you can feel poor with a W-2 over $350,000. Or $38 million!

Let me make a distinction about the need for money. Some money is necessary to provide for basic needs for survival: shelter, food, and medical care. Beyond that, a person earning $50,000 per year is just as "happy" as someone making $50,000,000 per year. Where does our attitude sour toward the financial spoke? Right after birth. We are fed downright lies throughout our lives about money. It's no wonder this spoke is broken throughout entire lifetimes. But it doesn't have to be. Let's dispel common misconceptions:

1. We've all heard: "Money is the root of all evil." It's a lie! I like George Bernard Shaw's quote: "Lack of money is the root of all evil."
2. People who win lotteries often live tragic lives that end in financial ruin.
3. Eighty-two percent of NFL athletes blow their savings and file for bankruptcy within two years of their last game.
4. Going broke doesn't help a homeless person. But financial abundance doesn't hurt a homeless person either—it may actually help.
5. Money doesn't grow on trees (actually, bills are made of trees).
6. The meek will inherit the earth.

Sound familiar? I could go on and on, but you get the picture. We have been fed so much depressing misinformation about money that it is no wonder we feed on anti-depressants by the billions.

Ready for a money metaphor? See it like water; some is necessary to survive but too much can drown you. Be grateful for what you have. A consciousness of gratitude will attract financial abundance. A consciousness of scarcity will keep you in the poorhouse.

The beauty of it all—and this applies to all six spokes—is that abundant prosperity and financial independence is a choice. Take a hard look at how you view your financial spoke; if you ranked it low, change the way you look at it starting right now.

Franklin D. Roosevelt said, "Happiness lies not in the mere possession of money; it lies in the joy of achievement, in the thrill of creative effort." Set creative goals for yourself like Wendy did and open the door to living the (financial abundance) dream.

Intellectual: I'm often asked how long it took to write this book. So I don't discourage anyone from writing, I usually say "three months." The real answer is *my whole lifetime*. Growing up with parents who read (and encouraged reading) all the time, I developed a desire to write a book at a young age. Earning an English degree in college further stoked my desire to write. But it wasn't until I started my own business that I decided to write this book. The practical part of this book (covered later) began roughly 20 years ago. After a few chapters, I lost interest. Call it writer's block, but I felt uninspired to finish.

Can you guess how I overcame writer's block? I did the unthinkable: I quit watching TV and discontinued my negative news newspapers. Then I read non-fiction books that I thought would inspire me. In a short time, I had devoured hundreds of books (the ones that inspired me the most are listed at the end of the book).

Mark Twain said, "The man who does not read good books has no advantage over the man who cannot read them." Profound. It was easier for Twain; in his day, there were no mindless TV programs to distract him. Twain was a voracious reader and guess where it got him? He was one of the brightest, most adored, and richest men of his time. If you want to write, you have to read; statistics also reveal that reading is directly proportional to wealth. See how the financial spoke overlaps the intellectual?

How did you answer the TV question earlier? The average

American household has a television on for nearly seven hours a day. That's almost a full-time job! I love people who tell me they don't (four-letter word) have enough time to read, exercise, etc., yet can couch potato for seven hours. I have a life coach client who sleeps with the TV on (or attempts to). Then she wonders why she feels drained when her alarm sounds. As much as 97% of our media has a negative bias, so is that what you really want to feed your brain— and subconscious? Who controls the remote control?

You are a genius. How does that statement make you feel? Do you agree? Most people do not. But it's true. You have limitless God-given intellectual potential, yet scientists assert you will only use between one and ten percent of your brain. Don't accept that for yourself. Treat your brain like a muscle and give it a workout. Beyond reading and writing every day, you can do plenty to stimulate your intellect: do puzzles, build something, debate other people, take a course, enroll in a seminar, learn about a different culture. The list is up to you, but set goals to unleash your genius within you.

Emotional: Emotion is energy in motion. Your energy (i.e., consciousness) is directly proportional to your results. And it all starts with your emotions. If you scored below 30 on the spokes, I guarantee you are in a negative frame of mind the majority of the time.

The Law of Attraction states that like attracts like. If you're depressed, guess what you'll get more of? Did you say bummed out? Don't fret if you really feel depressed; your emotions are in your control—they are a conscious choice. Remember, it takes only 17 seconds to raise your emotions.

I set a goal to be happy at least 95 percent of the time (it's not that hard). It starts with awareness. You have a God-given GPS built into your emotions. I'm not referring to the chatting monkey criticizing your every step—that's your brain going haywire. Your energy is set in motion through your gut instincts. When you follow your bliss, time stands still and you feel phenomenal. If you're not in a positive mood, you feel lousy. When your inner GPS causes you to feel good, the trick is to develop your awareness to stay there.

Positive emotions begin as soon as you awaken. Before I leave my bed, the first thing I do every single day is meditate for at least 15 minutes. I focus on gratitude, giving thanks for everything that pops in my head. After just 15 minutes, guess how I feel? Fantastic!

During the day, if something or someone bumps me off my path, I'm already programmed to handle it. I consciously say "Cancel" then think: "Negative thoughts, negative suggestions have no influence over me at any level of mind." If I notice stress rearing its ugly head at any time, this technique swats it away like the bug that it is.

Remember, there is no way to bliss; bliss is the way. When you are in a positive emotional state, positive results have to follow. It's universal law.

Physical: There are wonder chemicals that are naturally produced by your body. I call them "The Best Dope." Don't worry, they're legal and safe. In addition to making you feel good, they help you cope with stress. Interested?

For men, it's dopamine; for women, serotonin. Guess what all the anti-depressant drugs try to emulate? You got it: dopamine and serotonin. Contrary to popular belief, you don't have to take a pill to be happy (and suffer from nasty side effects). Exercise stimulates it. That's right. Only 20 minutes of exercise such as a vigorous walk produces 100 percent of your daily (and natural) happy drug.

In addition to exercise, what you ingest matters just as much. With all the diet plans out there, you don't need another one. Just cut out the white devils—sugar, salt, flour—and drink purified water all day. I gave up soda years ago and a funny thing happened: I lost weight and felt better.

In a given year, every cell inside you will die and be replenished by a new one. Think about this. You're given a new chance to rebuild yourself every moment. Regardless of your score, exercise and eat right—starting right now. No excuses.

Spiritual: You are a spiritual being living in a physical presence. Your spirit is eternal and is always connected to The Creator. Your spirit has domain over your mind which has domain over your body. But how much time do you spend on this essential spoke? If you are working for eight hours, watching TV for seven, eating for three, and sleeping for six, when does your spirit get to play?

Back to the GPS analogy, you feel the best when your spirit is allowed to play—when you follow your bliss. Enlightenment is a term that evades most people, yet it's within everyone's reach. Simply lighten your load of self-imposed limits and burdens, and when time stands still, you are in an enlightened state. Interviewers often ask me if "The Bliss List" is like "The Bucket List." I reply, "Yes, but in 'The Bliss List,' you don't have to die." This usually draws a laugh, but it's no joke: many people believe the only way to enlightenment is through dying. That's sad.

The easiest way to allow your spirit to play? Meditate. Do you see why I'm such a huge proponent of meditation? In only 15 minutes, the benefits of meditating far outweigh the detriments . . . because there aren't any! Find a peaceful place, close your eyes, quiet your chatting monkey, and feel your spirit rejoice.

Relational: We are meant to be relational beings, not reclusive. Yet, so many people have relationship problems—fighting with family, can't find a partner, feel belittled by bosses, disrespected by kids, etc. These are all very real challenges that we all face at some point. Forget all that for a moment.

Consider: the most important relationship you'll ever have is with yourself. You cannot love others unless you first love yourself. It

THE BLISS LIST   83

sounds cliché, but it's truly that simple. By self love, I'm not talking about conceit; this is about gratitude for the miracle your Creator has created. And that miracle is you. If this still sounds like a tired old cliché to you, lose that paradigm before it deteriorates more relationships.

You're probably asking, "Okay, but how can I love myself?" You've already started to make great strides. Just by writing and thinking about your own Bliss List, you are improving your relationship with yourself. Whenever you do something that makes you happy inside, you are in inner harmony. Like attracts like and harmony attracts— you guessed it—more harmony in all relationships. In Wendy's case, once she started to let go of petty grievances (and they're all petty), her relational spoke flourished—and in a short time.

The Bible mentions, "The kingdom of God is within" (more than once). "The kingdom of God" is not some buried treasure in a faraway cave. It is within you. Tap into your kingdom by thinking about what makes you happy. If you're happy, guess which types of people you're going to attract into your life?

Don't buy into the Jerry McGuire movie line, "You complete me." Baloney. You are already a miracle and you don't need anyone to finish your Creator's job. If you're in a positive state of mind the majority of the time, you'll be able to share the new, complete you. And, you'll attract people who will enhance your life, not try to complete it.

READY FOR A SIX SPOKES OF BLISS CHALLENGE?

I'm going to issue a challenge: quit TV for one week (you won't miss much). If there's a program you just can't miss, record it for later—but eliminate TV for seven days. Use the seven hours per day you save to read, write, meditate, pray, enjoy nature, listen to classical music, spend time with loved ones—and forgive those you hold a grudge against.

Use your free time to develop your Bliss Cards and Bliss Board. They magnify your focus on your spokes; the more you focus, the faster you manifest results. Though you hopefully have some ideas in mind, I'm going to make it even easier to start by giving you powerful mantras designed for each spoke. Commit to saying them throughout the day. Keep them on your wall, in your wallet/purse, in your car, in a frame on your desk, and any other place you are likely to look during your day:

> **Financial:** "Money flows easily and frequently."
>
> **Intellectual:** "Negativity has no influence over me."
>
> **Emotional:** "I choose peace in all things."
>
> **Physical:** "Every day, in every way, I'm getting better and better."
>
> **Spiritual:** "I am a spiritual being, always connected to my divine Creator."
>
> **Relational:** "I choose to love everyone, including myself."

After the week, if you notice improvement in your Six Spokes of Bliss (you will), then go for two weeks. Then three. In only three weeks you will have reprogrammed your brain—I promise. You will be astounded by the results.

Now, it's time for the practical—putting your desires into action by using your disciplined, positive mind.

4

Your Invisible
First Impression

Remember your decision about your first job? You spent a mere few hours or even minutes determining where you were going to spend the bulk of your waking time. Scary. Here's something even more scary. You'll spend even less time on one of the most important means for you to obtain your blissful dream job—your résumé.

You know the importance of a good first impression. Yet very few people spend enough time on their true first impression—their résumés. Believe me, I've seen plenty of lousy résumés—some I'll share soon. These people didn't think of their résumé as their first impression. This mindset (a real hindrance) will only keep them stuck in the mud and certainly not propel them into a blissful dream job.

Your résumé is your invisible first impression. And it goes without saying how important first impressions are.

THE ONE-PAGE MYTH

I had an executive level manager—we'll call him Jim—argue with me trying to defend his single-page (and inadequate) résumé. After college, he had worked for three blue-chip companies. He had a consistent track record of achievement and the promotions to show for it, accounting for a total of seven jobs in fourteen years of professional experience. Impressive background—and perfect for the job I was hoping to place him in.

Jim should have been a no-brainer for the Vice President job my firm was retained to fill. He had all the qualifications and then some—but they were not on paper. In my opinion, Jim had short-changed his career by shoe-horning it into a one-page résumé.

The result: I presented his résumé to my client whose first words were, "Looks light." (No kidding!)

Sometimes, that's all it takes to derail your opportunity to interview and lose a potential dream job. Since this particular client was a personal friend of many years, I attempted to push back with, "Oh, it's only a résumé. You will really like this guy!" I didn't sound too convincing.

"Who else do you have?" he replied with a disturbed tone.

There wasn't much more I could do except to slide Jim in with other candidates—later. I knew if I could just get him in front of the hiring manager, he would nail it—in spite of his lame résumé. This entire dilemma was due to a wimpy, one-page résumé—that created a poor first impression.

Unless you spend the time necessary to give yourself a positive first impression with an attention-grabbing résumé that rocks (I'll help make the process easier than you think), you may as well resign yourself to the fact that you'll never be given the opportunity. On my wall, I have a saying, "Success means being ready when opportunity knocks." Having the best résumé you possibly can is being ready for that opportunity and leads to success.

I'm frequently asked, "What is the best résumé format?" You could ask ten people this question and may very well get ten differ-ent answers. The best résumé is one that moves yours to the top of the pile with the hiring manager. How? After years of trial and error, I have formulated an ideal résumé format that works. First, I'll describe it and then later give you some examples and a template.

The best résumé covers two areas: (1) activities and (2) accomplishments in chronological order, beginning with your most recent job. Use sentences in paragraph form for the activities and bullet points to highlight your accomplishments.

Some résumé advisers say you should do your résumé in the form of a letter. My answer: if that's what your dream company wants, that's what you do, but the most widely accepted résumé is still done chronologically by job/company.

Many times, a recruiter may do his or her own "write up" about you in lieu of your résumé. Make it easy by having a strong chronological résumé with clear descriptions of what you do/did and what you accomplished. This should give a recruiter enough ammo to present your qualifications with enthusiasm.

Ready to begin? First off, don't feel as if you have to pay a résumé service to do your résumé for you. Résumé services tend to follow templates that lack individuality. Don't defer your dream job quest to an outside service. Write it yourself. Use Microsoft Word if you have it. Word is the most accepted business software and chances are, a résumé service would type it on Word anyway. As another bonus, doing it yourself gives you the very important option of altering and tailoring your content to fit your target dream companies.

When listing your name at the top of the first page, use your nickname (the name you go by) rather than your full legal name. This adds a little warmth to the start and avoids your having to ask the hiring manager to call you something else right off the bat (first impressions). There's a big difference in listing *Daniel Arthur Worthington, III* vs. *Dan Worthington.*

PARAGRAPH YOUR ACTIVITIES

This is the mundane but necessary part of your résumé.

- In the first line, describe your primary, overall responsibility. What geography you cover, how many employees you manage, any clients you are directly responsible for, and anything that may be pertinent to companies you are targeting. For example: *Responsible for $100 million in annual sales in the eastern United States for a 550-item pet food manufacturer.*

- Next, describe your company's reporting and operational structure. *Report to the Vice President of Sales, oversee a direct sales force at headquarters and a brokerage force at retail. Supervise 100 employees through eight direct reports: five Region Managers, two Divisional Category Managers and one Administrative Assistant.*

- If you are directly responsible for any customers, especially large, recognizable ones, indicate them by name.

- If you were able to obtain a position description for your target job, include anything that pertains to what the company is looking for in your background. Interject any applicable responsibilities accordingly. For example, if company x is looking for a people manager, include how many employees you manage and list their titles.

- Do not fill your paragraph with flowery verbiage such as *while keeping the company's best interests in mind.* Keep it clear and concise. Fewer syllables wins you points with the interviewer.

BULLET POINT YOUR ACCOMPLISHMENTS

Bullet points are the most important element of your entire résumé. And, ironically, typically the format item most résumé writers forget to use. Any time you can use objects in a presentation (a résumé is a presentation of you), the impact is far greater than merely with words. The reader is more likely to remember items highlighted with an object.

Your Advertising 101 class taught you that, ideally, you would use colored objects in a presentation, but, like the objects example, that's not sound advice for your résumé. Notwithstanding colored objects, bullet points are effective and easy to use (one click on the old toolbar). They draw the reader to your accomplishments. Using my bullet-point advice will catapult your résumé to the must-see pile.

What is it you want to bullet point? Accomplishments such as these:

- Increases in revenue (if double digit—more on this in a minute)
- Decreases in expenses
- Awards won
- Bonuses earned
- Rank vs. peers (especially if it's a #1)
- New innovative technique(s) designed by you and used by others
- Buzz words important to the target company
- Leadership/task forces, especially if chosen by senior management
- Teamwork

- Hiring, promoting employees
- Restructuring to improve efficiency

Bullet points must be believable yet impressive. How can you make them believable? Quantify and qualify—and without any passive words. Avoid using words such as *implement, execute,* or *follow.* The language in your bulleted accomplishments should reflect strength and confidence. Use these strong words: *created, designed, led, obtained, ranked #1, awarded,* and so on. The following is a bullet-point example:

- Implemented sales programs

versus

- Increased sales by 31.6% in FY 2008, +37.3% in FY 2007, and +32.1% in FY 2006

Which bullet point is more effective? "Implemented sales programs" is too vague and is something anyone could say. It says, "I drop off the stuff other people wrote for me to say." In short: it underwhelms the reader.

The second bullet point quantifies (31.6%, 37.3%, and 32.1%) and qualifies (FY 2008, 2007, 2006). It is believable because of its precision and it is impressive—you always want to use double digits for increases.

What if you didn't have double digit increases? Well, you have to be creative. Not many employers say, "Get me some salespeople who can drive some stagnant, single-digit increases." Let's say your increases were a modest +3.2% in '08, +4.2% in '07 and +3.8% in '06. Your bullet point would be

- Increased sales by 11.2% vs. industry average of +5.1%

I would advise you to leave out the three singular years and instead add them together, since you were in the job three years. And we added the "industry average" number, so the reader can see you more than doubled the industry average. It is truthful, and just as impressive and believable (quantified and qualified). Much more so than "Implemented sales programs."

Tailor your accomplishments to your target company's hot buttons. Place yourself in their shoes and brainstorm your most applicable successes. Be creative. List them in order of importance, with the top bullet point being the most important.

Which ones are the most important? The accomplishments most sought after by all companies are:

- Increasing revenues
- Decreasing expenses
- Increasing efficiencies

For people working in a creative capacity instead of sales/operations, list projects, products, inventions or patents you developed in addition to working within and hopefully under budget.

I'm going to repeat this point from earlier:

- Quantify and qualify
- Be specific
- Avoid flowery verbiage
- Use action verbs

Be deliberate in marketing yourself. If you seek a position that will emphasize people development, list the number of employees you have developed and promoted.

Try to limit the number of bullet points to five for your most recent (and most important) position and three or fewer for earlier positions. Don't dilute your bullet points. Less is more here. Five impactful bullet points stand out and get the reader excited; eleven blend in and lose their impact, not to mention the reader.

The average time the interviewer will spend on your résumé is less than one minute. Less than one minute! Hit home runs with your bullet points. Ask your executive recruiter, "What is most important to the hiring manager?" and tailor your bullet points accordingly.

A candidate once told me—in trying to defend his weak résumé (and the fact that he was too lazy to re-do it)—that he didn't want to "give too much information on the résumé, or there wouldn't be anything to talk about in the interview." Wrong-O! A lousy résumé won't get you the interview. If properly written, though, a résumé can allow you to focus on chemistry with the interviewer versus explaining (that is, defending) your background. The following tips will help your résumé shine:

LENGTH

If you follow the recommended chronological, paragraph, and bullet point format, your résumé should be as long as it needs to be. One-page résumés place you at a disadvantage, yet some people still believe a résumé should be one page. Candidates with one page résumés rarely get hired in six figure jobs.

The one-pager is realistic for a recent college graduate; the more experience you have, the longer your résumé should be—even if you've been in the same job for years. Your accomplishments should match your time in a job, especially for your most recent work experience listed. If your résumé is clear, concise, and well-written, length should be a non-issue. So, length really doesn't matter (just wanted to see if you were still alert).

CONTENTS

Sections entitled "Objectives" and "Career Summaries" are redundant and do not belong on a résumé. The only exception might be if you are trying to change industries. Either way, a well-written cover letter should serve as your career summary. The very fact that you are interested in this particular position means it is your objective.

Your résumé should include these headings:

- Professional Experience
- Education (all degrees—undergraduate and graduate, with grades listed if at least or higher than 3.0/4.0)
- Honors (if applicable)
- Professional Affiliations (if applicable)
- Additional Training
- Personal (optional)

If you are lucky enough to uncover that your target dream company is looking for a well-adjusted employee (defined as married with children in business circles), by all means, list it; the flip side is just as many employers look for unattached candidates (single, divorced, or empty nest married) who will be open to travel and relocation. People like to hire in their own likeness, so try to find as much as you can about who's interviewing you and take a calculated risk on your personal information.

If you're living in a van down by the river and are thrice divorced, do not include.

SOME RÉSUMÉ DON'TS

No picture of yourself (I've seen people include this!) and no flowery verbiage. As a rule, if it can be stated with fewer words and syllables, do it. Think technical writing here. Don't use colored paper or cheap copier paper. White 100% cotton, watermarked paper (usually called "résumé paper" at retailers like Targer, OfficeMax, Staples, and Office Depot) is always a winner.

A confusing résumé, littered with typos, will land you in the round file (aka the waste basket). Fast. Take the time to proofread your résumé before it is printed! One of the best resources available is already in your computer—spell-check. Use it.

Don't think spell-check alone will suffice. You need to go over your résumé with a fine-tooth-comb, word for word. Yours truly sent out 750 résumés to all of my targeted recruiting firms with the word *manger*. Guess what? Spell-check let it go because *manger* is a word. But *manger* would have better described the nativity scene than the fact that I was a *manager*. Oops!

My eyes alone didn't catch this glaring typo. So in addition to your careful proofreading, ask trusted colleagues and friends to critique your résumé for you. You only get one chance, and your first impression has to be perfect.

A RÉSUMÉ THAT WORKS

The following "sample" résumé is an actual one (with names changed) of a person I placed at the VP level with a Fortune 500 company.

Though I thought her résumé was a little wordy, it worked. The content of responsibilities and accomplishments was an ideal match for my client's needs. In fact, the VP of HR called me immediately after she received the combination of my write up with Sharon's résumé. She enthusiastically asked, "When can we see this candidate? She looks perfect!" I love it when that happens. And Sharon was perfect for the job. She nailed it! At the time, it was my most lucrative placement.

SHARON REVENUE

123 Success Lane Anyexit, New Jersey 08888 • (908)123-4567 (H) • (908) 123-4568 (W)

PROFESSIONAL EXPERIENCE

Phenomenal Products, Liberty Corner, New Jersey   June 1992–Present

Director of Trade Marketing, Footcare Division   March 1994–Present

Responsible for P&L management of an eight-figure U.S. Trade Spending Budget and Program Development in a $258 million division. Report to the Vice President of Sales and supervise eight employees: one Trade Marketing Manager, three Regional Trade Marketing Managers, two Category Analysts, one Shelf Analyst and one Administrative Assistant. Provide strategic leadership and analytical direction to increase volume and profitability through effective Account Based Marketing.

- Through optimizing our Trade P&L, increased category growth by +8% (114% greater than total HBC) while reducing trade expenses by $663 thousand.
- Developed a Category Management initiative for the Footcare Category with a focus on item optimization. This program resulted in 188 new distributions in our top 25 customers, generating an incremental $14 million annually.
- Led a multi-functional team in the development of our annual trade and consumer plan. Our promotional effectiveness initiative is designed to increase brand equity.
- Restructured the department by hiring six of eight employees. Promoted three employees from entry level analyst positions to District Manager, Category Business Analyst and Supervisor, Shelf Analysis. Upgraded five of the eight positions to incorporate more talent and experience.

West Region Manager, Footcare Division   June 1992–Feb. 1994

Responsible for $30 million in the 12 Western States from Colorado to Hawaii. Supervised 35 employees: three District Managers who managed 17 Territory Managers in our direct sales business; two Broker Managers who supervised nine Brokers and two Distributors. Directly responsible for the Safeway Corporate account.

- Achieved +19% growth in 1993 highlighted by 125% attainment of new products volume objective.
- Delivered a net gain of 256 new items into distribution, resulting in $2 million in incremental annual sales.
- Increased the Footcare Category by 10%, outpacing the national average by 43%.
- Ranked #1 in market share and factory sales growth in 1992 versus peer group.

- Led a major restructure in an upgrade of talent while reducing expenses by $600 thousand. Hired five employees and promoted one District Manager and two Territory Managers.
- Achieved full distribution at each Safeway Division for a major new products launch through a strategic alliance with Safeway Corporate.

The Promote and Gamble Distribution Company   April 1980–April 1992

District Manager, Grocery Retail Ops   Jan. 1991–April 1992

Responsible for over $1 billion in retail sales for the Company's Food/Beverage, Soap and Paper divisions with budgets totaling $4 million. Managed the Los Angeles District including Southern California, Arizona, and Nevada during the first full year of implementation. Responsible for a staff of 50 employees: five Unit Managers, two Market Field Managers, one Shelf Analyst, one Marketing Manager, one Administrative Assistant and 40 Sales Representatives.

At the end of this book, in a section called Résumé Makeovers, I share some actual résumés from people with whom I have worked. I will show the "before" and "after" to help illustrate the differences between a résumé that will get placed in the round file (usually crumpled up) versus those moved to the top of the pile. Though the names have been altered, the basic content is verbatim.

5

I Have a Killer Résumé, Now What?

Once you've developed a killer résumé, and you feel confident that potential employers will be equally impressed, it's time to market yourself.

"What is the best marketing strategy?" I'm often asked by candidates. That's a loaded question to ask a recruiter—a "headhunter" will usually just say, "Work exclusively with me!" That's not what is best for you though. You don't ask a barber if you need a haircut. You don't ask a stock broker if you need to change your portfolio. So don't ask a headhunter for advice on your marketing strategy (I'll discuss working with recruiters in the next chapter).

The best marketing strategy is this:

- Network, network, network
- Direct mail/e-mail targeted dream companies
- Direct mail/e-mail targeted executive recruiters

Networking plays the most important practical part in finding your ideal job. Contrary to the digital age trends, networking is NOT online (i.e., passive). Popping out a few e-mails and applying to company website job postings is not networking; it usually lands you in cyber-storage. Effective networking is in person. It takes time and energy, but pays exponentially in the most important return on investment—your dream job. (This is not to say that online networking can't be useful, but you need to use it carefully, thoughtfully, and in concert with your other efforts. See the section below for tips on how to do it effectively.)

Let me take the fear (four-letter word) out of networking. Think of people you know and how they can help you: former bosses, colleagues, classmates, alumni, friends, family, neighbors, members of organizations (both social and professional), and members of your religious affiliation. The trick is to cast a wide net. Now, develop a plan to visit them in person. And bring copies of your résumé along. The more effectively you network, the more likely your bliss occupation will happen—don't sit back and expect it to present itself to you.

Passive job strategies don't cut it, especially in this ultra-competitive job market. By this, I'm talking about online applications—especially when you have an "in." Applying via a company website is just about as likely to land you a dream job as buying a lottery ticket will make you a multi-millionaire. I understand it's not practical to meet every contact you have in person, but make a concerted effort for personal contact.

You may feel awkward reaching out to someone you haven't spoken to in a while. Don't. Realize you don't have to go for the jugular immediately by making it obvious you are calling for a job. Finesse a network contact with a non-threatening, "I'd like to have coffee or breakfast with you," and don't even mention your desire to work there. Keep it social—at first. You can always broach the subject of your job hunt while relaxing with a latte.

Usually every company is tied—either directly or indirectly—to professional organizations. They offer events that are ideal networking opportunities. A person's LinkedIn page usually lists professional organizations and affiliations. Most people don't take the time to do this basic research.

Once you are set to attend an event, dress professionally, bring printed résumés, and sell yourself, while the unemployed sit home blasting their e-résumé into cyberspace.

ADD A KILLER COVER LETTER

Regarding direct mail (snail mail) and e-mail, prepare a professional one-page cover letter that you will attach to your new killer résumé. In this case, length does matter; make it no more than a few paragraphs. Mark Twain said, "I didn't have time to send a short letter so I'm writing you a long one instead." Take the time. Being concise and precise in your cover letter is as important as a killer résumé. Don't bog it down with clutter about your past experiences. This is not the time to duplicate (and regurgitate) what's already in your résumé. Think hook, line, and sinker.

What is the best way to interest the recipient of your letter? How can you hook him or her—to place your résumé on the top of the pile and not in the round file? Starting with a personal connection you made with the hiring manager is a great opening. If that hasn't happened, develop an attention-grabbing opening that mentions an advantage you have as a potential employee.

Next, what's your line to the top? If you can, mention an inside connection—"I was referred by so-and-so, whom you respect." Your chances of being seen greatly improve.

And the sinker? Always provide vital related experiences and advantages that you bring to the hiring manager and the target company (but keep it short!).

A couple key tips about what to do with your killer cover letter:

- Send your letter to the highest ranking person you can—ideally, the chairman or CEO. The top-down approach works magically—even though the chairman likely isn't to be the person who is responsible for interviewing and hiring you, having the chairman forward your information with his or her approval (either directly or implied) gets you seen. Usually quickly.

- Never, ever, send direct mail with no name or title (do not say this: *To: HR Department)* or with the ever-lame *To Whom It May Concern*. It is a sure-fire way to get tossed in the round file.

E-MAIL OR SNAIL MAIL?

Which is better: direct mail or e-mail?

E-mail is actually a more effective way than sending a letter through the regular mail to market yourself to a dream company. Most managers at least glance at each e-mail; whereas, direct mail is more likely to be stacked somewhere—for a prolonged period.

But there is an even more creative way to reach someone: send via FedEx. Almost every FedEx package is opened and read by the recipient. It is expensive (compared to a postage stamp) but very effective. Delivery-service letters and packages (whether DHL, FedEx, or UPS, even USPS Express Mail) require a signature that gets your direct mail in the right person's hands.

Most hiring managers feel that if someone shelled out $20 to $30 to FedEx them a letter and résumé, it must be important enough to read. Getting your résumé in the hands of the intended person is the purpose. If landing you an ideal job costs you $30, isn't the return on investment worth it?

If you send a hard copy (snail mail or FedEx) first, then follow-up via e-mail a week or two later. Attach both your original cover letter and résumé and mention it in your document. Both direct mail and electronic mail are effective ways to market yourself, but the combination is even better. This is true whether you are targeting a dream company directly or trying to reach an executive search firm. Regarding the attachment, both Word and PDF docs are acceptable. The advantage with a PDF over Word doc is it is always uniform and can't be changed. If you're using Word, make sure you save it in compatibility mode in case your recipient has a different version.

What about applying through the target company's website? If you are applying for a specific opening that was listed on the website, go for it. You will not reach the chairman—more likely your letter and résumé will land in the Inbox of a junior human resources person, but it's worth a try. A better approach is applying through the website and then referencing the opening you saw with a targeted FedEx to a senior manager. As I mentioned earlier, this is a passive strategy and one that should only be used if you cannot get a face-to-face or direct phone contact.

Don't get discouraged if your phone doesn't ring off the hook after a direct mail/e-mail marketing effort. The replies you receive will be less than 5 percent on average; remember, the wider you effectively cast your net, the more likely you will be to land that blissful dream job. Ready for some practical advice?

HOW TO PRESENT YOURSELF ONLINE— *TO TWEET OR NOT TO TWEET, THAT IS THE QUESTION!*

Can social media help you obtain your dream job? Yes and no.

First, a word of caution about social networking: every tweet, post, picture, blog, and/or comment can be viewed by your future dream job hiring manager—with nightmarish consequences. Smart phones can make dumb postings online, with typos or emotionally charged words (that you'll regret later). If this gave you a sudden thump in your chest, that was my intention. I have seen people derail their chances of getting hired via misuse of Facebook and Twitter.

Don't panic, no need to delete your Facebook account; you can still utilize social networking. Effective online marketing has landed plenty of dream jobs. Use the following seven tips:

1. **Become a multiple personality.** Not the disorder, but create two personas: personal and business, and keep them strictly separate. Just like there are two versions of yourself in an interview—the professional answer versus how you'd answer with your buddies—there are also two of you online. The easiest way to do this? Look to LinkedIn for business purposes and Facebook and Twitter for personal use. Unless you can promise you'll only tweet with the professional you (be honest now), never use your real name as your Twitter ID. If you have a side job or do volunteer work (I'm a Big Brother, Big Sister volunteer sponsor), it's

okay to list in LinkedIn. Avoid religious and/or political affiliations though.

2. **Watch your privacy settings.** To tell you not to use Facebook or other social media sites is unreasonable. But, use the privacy settings so your interviewer doesn't get to see the posted picture of you in your Halloween costume under a beer bong (or much worse).

3. **Screen postings.** As a rule, if you wouldn't want a potential employer to read it, don't write it. That includes what others (friends?) have posted. Monitor postings on a daily basis and delete anything that breaks our rule. The great thing about the Internet is also a detriment to a job applicant—it's largely unregulated. It's a good idea to Google yourself before applying, because that's the first step most interviewers take. You need to think like a marketer and the brand is you. Personal branding projects a professional image and can assist rather than hinder you. It's very easy to develop a personal brand but just as easy to destroy it with a few misguided tweets, postings, blogs, and even comments. Be careful what you "Like."

4. **Promote your personal brand using LinkedIn**—an online source utilized by most executive recruiters, human resources professionals, and hiring managers. First, set up a professional profile picture and brief profile, then build your friends through your networking list. Ask key individuals in your network to write a recommendation of your work (use these in your Brag Book—discussed

later). Do not insert your entire résumé, only general highlights. And no typos. Hiring managers will often check your LinkedIn page. It has yet to happen to one of my candidates, but I've heard horror stories about hiring managers canceling interviews because the candidate falsified his or her background (usually by omitting a job on the résumé that appears on LinkedIn).

5. **Stand out.** Anyone can set up a LinkedIn account (it's free), but not everyone uses it to differentiate and establish credibility. Demonstrate you're an expert in a particular field or subject. Align yourself with strong content and share it with others by answering questions on user forums. LinkedIn's Answers application is a great place to put this into practice. Constantly scour through questions that other LinkedIn members have posted in your area of expertise or search by keyword. The more high quality answers you provide, the more visible you become.

6. **Target your marketing.** Compile a list of companies you've got in your sights, find out who works there and, if possible, who's in charge of hiring. Then make friends with or follow them on social-networking sites. Many corporate sites list personnel with names, faces, and a bio (very helpful info to network). Search LinkedIn for company names and double check with a search of PeekYou, Plaxo and Spoke (other useful social media directories aimed at business users). Soon, you will develop an extensive list of names; you can make friends with people on all these networks (professional page on Facebook only).

7. **Consider whether you need a website, blog, or a YouTube video.** It depends. If you can establish yourself as an expert in your field or target field, by all means. Again, be the professional you for every image and comment. You can develop an online brag book or portfolio with videos of you being interviewed on TV or reprint of an article you contributed to, etc. Though I have seen several online résumés (short videos), unless you can afford high quality sound, lighting, and photography, don't do it.

A final word concerning an online strategy: the best networking is always in person. Use social media to help you set up informal meetings. I've seen many, "Let's get a coffee sometime," turn into, "Why don't you come to work for me?"

CONTROL THE CONTROLLABLES

What are controllables? They are creating the most professional and effective cover letter and résumé that you possibly can, researching whom you should send it to, and where it should be sent.

Most companies have a web page that contains the mailing address, e-mails, and information about the management team by title. Plan on sending your cover letter and résumé to the highest ranking person in your target company.

The following is a sample cover letter to be sent to an employer:

Shelly Johnson
110 First Way
Alexandria, VA 22306
(802) 555-5544
Shelly.Johnson@home.com

Mr. Henry Fodora
Ideal Company, Inc.
100 Fifth Avenue
New York, NY 10001

Dear Mr. Fodora,

Nancy Smith of Golden Associates Advertising suggested I contact you regarding the possible public relations opening in your firm.

As an editor and writer for Alexandria's city magazine, I've developed my talent and experience as a public relations writer. Because the staff is very small, I've worn a number of hats, including developing the editorial format and individual story concepts, writing numerous articles, editing copy, laying out the magazine, and supervising production.

Prior to my current position, I was highly involved in the public relations industry, working for Handley & Pratt, where I prepared numerous press releases and media guides, as well as managing several major direct mail campaigns.

My high degree of motivation has been recognized by my previous employers who have quickly promoted me to positions of greater responsibility. I was promoted from assistant editor to editor of *Alexandria Monthly* after only six months.

I am eager to talk with you about the contribution I could make to your firm. I will call you the week of May 21st to see if we can find a mutual time and date to get together and discuss the possibility.

Your consideration is greatly appreciated.

Cordially,
Shelly Johnson

By all means, send a killer cover letter with your résumé even if there is no posted opening. If you do not receive a response within two weeks, call to follow up. Leave only one voicemail message, but keep calling until the employer answers the phone. Be prepared for a mini-interview.

Finally, employ what you learned in the first section of this book: use visualization. See the recipient of your letter reading it and reaching for the phone to call you right away. Then, see and feel how excited you are to receive a job offer. Use visualization to focus your positive thinking on obtaining your bliss. The result is worth much more than the effort.

6

Don't Call Us
Headhunters

I offer a unique perspective on executive recruiters. Why? Because I am one. I have been living my dream as president of an executive search firm for almost 20 years. Even better, I have been on both sides of the desk as interviewer and interviewee.

Job searchers often ask me, "How did you become a recruiter?" Ironically, it was while working as an employee, and later as an employer, that I began to desire to enter the world of recruiting.

I was fortunate to have gained these interesting perspectives throughout my 31-year career (so far, and I'm far from even thinking about retiring). While I was with a Fortune 100 company, it publicly announced that the division I was in was being divested, so the company had a reason to help us land other employment (and they paid for it). For the first time in my career, I was able to talk to every recruiter that I possibly could without hurting my career. My bosses even referred me to recruiters.

In about seven months, I was able to speak to over 200 recruiters. Of those, I found only two that I had any professional respect for. Some were downright tacky. I had one call my wife "Toots" (I'm not joking, and she sure didn't think it was funny!). You can usually tell in the first few minutes if the recruiter is professional or not.

At the time, the average recruiting firm earned over $375,000 per year—many were one- or two-person shops. The money was good, yet the level of service was poor: lousy follow-up, lack of understanding of the client or the position, and poor communication skills. I said, "Hmm, I can do that." And about three years later, I did!

I had an advantage that many so-called headhunters didn't have. I had experience and training in staffing, managing (but not *manging*), and building businesses. Every job I would recruit for, I had already done. Being a Vice President with a Fortune 500 (#31) company gave me instant credibility with candidates and clients. Many of the headhunters had never done anything else other than paper-pushing and headhunting in their lives—and it was obvious!

Tip #1: Don't call a recruiter a *headhunter* if you want him or her to actually help you. Use the term *recruiter* or, better still, *executive search consultant.*

Every job has seemingly morphed into euphemisms. Stewardess became Flight Attendant; Used Car Salesman became Previously Owned Vehicle Sales Executive; and Cashiers became Client Service Representatives. Executive recruiters are still referred to as headhunters. Some even call themselves that. I like to think of myself as a Mystic Career Guide and Life Coach and, thanks to this book, instead of author or writer, I'm now an Inspirational Written-Entertainment Facilitator.

TYPES OF RECRUITERS

Many years ago recruiters were paid by the job seeker (that is, by the candidate). The recruiter would be paid by the candidate, usually up front, to "market" the candidate and then send the résumé to every company he or she knew who could possibly employ the candidate.

Today, that strategy has changed. Recruiters are paid by the hiring company (turn and run if a headhunter tries to charge you). Recruiters are generally categorized by the way they are paid, either with an up front retainer or after the placement is made on a contingency.

There are more than 5,000 recruiters. It doesn't matter how the recruiter is paid: both retained and contingency recruiters could hold your blissful dream job on their turbo-charged computer. As a general rule of thumb, retained recruiters work on more senior-level jobs (director level on up), and contingency recruiters cover the gamut, but generally work on the junior (director level on down).

I have worked on both contingency and retainer, but, for the past eight years, nearly all my work has been done on retainer (or, in rare instances, on exclusive contingency). Regardless of which recruiter type, you want a recruiter possessing strong relationships with companies that you are targeting—these are your dream companies. Usually, this means your recruiter is working on an exclusive arrangement.

You should always ask your recruiter what his or her relationship is to the company: *Are you working on retainer or contingency? Is the agreement exclusive?* If not, ask how many other recruiters are being used for the search.

Ask: *How did your relationship with this company start?* Look for a relationship with senior management and length of time of over two years. *How many placements have you made with this company?* (Look for more than one. You don't want to be the guinea pig.) These are important questions to ferret out the paper-pushers from the professional recruiters.

Many companies have their own in-house recruiters. They are paid a salary and usually receive a bonus. All of their work is done for the same company, so they will probably not be looking for what's right for you; rather, they will typically try to sell you on their company as the only place you should consider. Bear this in mind when they offer you career advice. It will be obvious that their advice is myopic and biased, but that's okay. Many times, companies who have in-house recruiters still will contract third-party (that is, outside) recruiters.

Ideally, your recruiter will have an exclusive relationship with the company he or she is representing and then all you have to do is to get to the top of the pile of the recruiter's extensive list of possible candidates (more on that soon).

HOW TO FIND RECRUITERS

Word-of-mouth is a good starting point. Ask your network of friends and business associates if they can recommend an executive recruiter. Beyond your networking efforts, *The Directory of Executive Recruiters* by Kennedy Publications is a great resource for locating recruiters. Aptly referred to as the "red book" (it's always had a red cover,) this directory categorizes recruiters by retained (my firm is listed there) and contingency. Remember, both are acceptable and either type could potentially hold your dream job.

In the red book (found in most major bookstores and libraries and on Amazon, but consult the most recent edition—updated annually), you can search by geography and function, so you can focus your reach to recruiters who specialize in the industries you are targeting. The red book gives you the firm's name, a key contact name (usually the owner/president), phone number, e-mail, and mailing address.

It's best to try to reach the key contact via telephone, but don't get discouraged if you don't get through; your next step is to send an e-mail or a snail mail hard copy with a brief but professional note detailing your background and desired job and geographic preferences.

If you include a copy of your résumé, make sure you write, "Please do not present my qualifications without my prior approval" on your cover letter. This is necessary to protect yourself from headhunters (those numbskulls who earn the title headhunter) who don't have your best interests at heart. For example, some headhunters will "float" your résumé in to a company—in other words, send in your background (and claim a stake on a fee as high as 40 percent of your first year's total compensation) without you even knowing, let alone approving, the company.

This gets particularly sticky if you have targeted the company directly (on your own) and have been able to get introduced to the company (without the use of a recruiter), only to find that some headhunter has sent (floated) your résumé in to the same company—unbeknownst to you.

If the company didn't budget for a recruiter fee, this could eliminate your candidacy through no fault of your own. Be leery of the recruiter who wants your résumé without telling you about a specific opportunity including the company's name. Floaters are not helpers in your job search.

Some recruiters will take shortcuts by floating your résumé in mass quantities, hoping they'll nail an easy fee by claiming a stake on you, even if this may cost you your ideal job. Some recruiters are "aligned" with other recruiters, either with a professional network or as partners (meaning they split the fee for a candidate placement with another recruiter). You can see how your résumé can appear all over the place—quickly and without your knowledge.

Imagine you are employed and your résumé gets in the wrong hands (your boss!) and you had no idea. Don't worry. As long as you protect yourself and treat your résumé as a sacred document by being very careful about where it is sent, you are okay. When you write, "Please do not present my qualifications without my prior approval," you also protect yourself from floaters.

Do not ever post your résumé on any online service. If you must use an online service, give sketchy details about your background and don't list your identity. Recruiters search online for résumés—you could have a bounty on your head from someone you have never even met.

My intention is not to scare you from working with recruiters—there are several highly competent and honest executive recruiters, and you should reach out to them and develop a strong relationship with the ones you trust. The purpose of this chapter is to educate you on the inner workings of recruiters—the behind-the-scenes stuff you don't usually learn about—until it's too late.

As with a prospective employer cover letter, keep your executive recruiter letter to one page. The following is a sample cover letter to be sent to an executive recruiter:

Karen Peoples
21 Money St.
Mt. Laurel, NJ 08054
609.555.0200
E-Mail: karen.peoples@home.com

Ms. Mabel Bodie
Able Employment Recruitment
3400 Einstein Parkway
Princeton, NJ 08540

Dear Ms. Bodie:

If you have a client seeking a brand strategist who can deliver bottom-line results, I'd like to make a strong case for myself. My track record in business-to-business international branding and marketing has helped enhance the reputations of such firms as Chase Manhattan, The New York Stock Exchange, AT&T, and

---

Microsoft, to name a few. I am contacting you as I believe it is time for a change. My employer is in the process of merging with another company, so I am actively exploring outside opportunities.

Of particular interest to your client firms:

I have demonstrated my strategic ability through successfully launching companies, communications departments, web sites, PR programs, ad campaigns, branding programs, and more.

I have consistently contributed my leadership skills in a corporate setting, while managing the creative process, motivating and empowering team members, fine-tuning marketing plans, and juggling multiple projects. I am a proficient top achiever and profit-minded leader.

My initiatives have resulted in increased awareness and press coverage, successful advertising campaigns, and winning branding strategies.

I am particularly interested in positions in the New York area that start at a salary range of $80K to $100K, in the following categories: marketing partner at a venture capital firm, entailing leveraging marketing opportunities for the portfolio companies and advising them on branding and marketing strategies; brand strategist and global head of marketing for a service-oriented preferably global business; senior-management role in a mid-sized integrated agency specializing in advertising, PR, and interactive services; marketing and communications head for a high-end financial services boutique; high-end headhunter or right-hand in a large philanthropic organization.

I'd like to meet with you to discuss adding value to one of your client firms as I've done for my previous employers. *Please do not present my qualifications without my prior approval.* I'll contact you soon to arrange a meeting. Should you wish to contact me before then, I can be reached during the day on my direct line (609.555.6300) or at home most evenings (609.555.0200).

Sincerely,
Karen Peoples

SOME DOS
FOR DEALING WITH A RECRUITER

When you get a recruiter "live" on the phone or, even better, face-to-face in a meeting, the following advice should help you gain points with him or her:

- Treat all of your communication with a recruiter as though he or she were the hiring manager.

- Always be professional. View each interaction as if you were on an interview—it usually is. I am continually forming my opinions about a candidate each time we interact.

- Be clear and concise about your background. Recruiters can size you up quickly by your ability to verbalize your thoughts in a clear, concise manner.

- Be honest and forthright about what you want to do. What are your goals? The only way a recruiter can help you is for you to clearly describe your ideal job. If the position and/or company the recruiter is pitching to you is not right, say so, and give your reason(s) in a professional, polite manner. Sometimes, turning down a job opportunity the right way can lead to the next call when your true blissful dream job becomes available.

- Be helpful. If the position is not right for you, try to recommend someone else. This will elevate your status with any recruiter.

SOME DON'TS
FOR DEALING WITH A RECRUITER

- Don't call to ask, "Did you get my résumé?" If you e-mailed it and it is in your sent folder, he or she received it.

- Don't ask a recruiter to do your résumé for you. Your résumé needs to be impressive on its own. Let the recruiter offer you advice on how to enhance your résumé to tailor it to the dream company's hot buttons. Graciously accept his or her advice, and if you agree, integrate it into your résumé.

- Don't overstay your welcome. Be mindful that recruiters are on the phone all day long with a stack of calls to make. Speaking "live" with a recruiter is a fairly rare occurrence. You gain points by being concise and direct.

- Don't call him or her *headhunter* even if he or she does. Always call him or her an *executive recruiter* (or, in my case, Mystic Career Guide and Life Coach . . . just wanted to see if you are paying attention).

- Don't expect a recruiter to tell you about more than one job that matches your background. They will usually try to sell you on the one that is the easiest fit for them or the most pressing at the time, even if it's not the best fit for you.

- Don't lie about previous employers, salary history, or education degrees. Ever!

- Don't call recruiters too often. Touching base once a month is usually about right. Weekly (and, especially, daily) calls become annoying and are usually screened and eventually ignored.

A good recruiter will stay in touch with you from time to time, especially if he or she has graded you an "A player" (topnotch candidate). My firm uses a subjective grading system in order like grades in school (A, A-, B+, B, B-, C+, and C). Following the advice you've just read should help you earn an "A." "C" players don't land ideal jobs and aren't in my database.

HOW CAN I GET ON THE "A" LIST?

The following tips will help:

- **Be organized.** Have good, clear, and concise thoughts and questions. Treat the recruiter as if he or she were the hiring manager. In some cases, they are.

- **Be available.** Recruiters (myself included) usually work at warp speed—making hundreds of calls in a given day. A recruiter's perception of time is equivalent to dog years. Be responsive: return a recruiter's phone call as soon as possible—even if it's to say you cannot talk until later, and schedule a time and date when you both will be available. Failure to return a call within 24 hours says, "I'm not interested."

- **Do the research.** Check out the company online, talk to customers, network—do everything you can to show that you are truly interested in the opportunity.

- **Ask good questions.** Do your own research and prepare good questions. Asking the recruiter pertinent and well-thought-out questions gives the recruiter confidence you will do well on an interview (remember, you are treating the recruiter as if he or she were the hiring manager).

- **Be professional.** Even if the recruiter is not professional (and many do give the profession a well-earned bad name), don't be unprofessional yourself.

- **Be honest.** If you have already taken another job, say so. Express thanks to the recruiter for thinking of you, but be direct and forthright.

- **Be helpful.** If you are not interested in the job the recruiter is selling, say so, and give your honest reasons, but always try to give recommendations of people you think could do the job. Being a good source elevates your "grade," and you are more likely to get the call on a better job next time.

- **Set up a network.** For the "good" recruiter you meet, stay in contact with him or her. Develop and foster a strong relationship. Try establishing your own personal network of recruiters you know and trust. There are a handful of candidates who have stayed in contact with me for over 15 years—I just placed one in a dream job.

If a recruiter has a job with an interesting company that sounds exciting to you, and says he or she would like to "present you" (in other words, the recruiter will e-mail your résumé with a brief cover note to his or her client), express enthusiasm, and ask as many questions as you can. Most recruiters know their client well both personally and professionally (I consider my clients my friends) and can give you pertinent information to integrate into your résumé and interview strategy.

Treating your recruiter with respect and demonstrating strong interpersonal skills will pay dividends and move you closer to your ideal job. I have many "A" candidates whom I have placed more than once and who always hear about the best jobs I am working on. Use this advice and forge some strong relationships. Put your strong recruiter network to work for you.

7
That All-Important Interview

Not so fast. Let's start long before the interview. I'll call this phase the pre-interview, because the more prepared for the interview you are, the more likely it is you will get that blissful dream job. Here are three things you need to do:

- Prepare
- Prepare
- Prepare

Get the picture? You cannot over-prepare for an interview. You need to know as much as you can about the prospective company, its culture, its history, and its challenges, which you will be asked to help solve. Also you need to know as much as possible about the position for which you are interviewing: why it is open, the background of the person you would report to—plus likes/dislikes, hot buttons, and management style. I know I am being redundant here, but preparation is the gateway to success.

An executive recruiter should know all of this information and should be more than willing to share it with you; the better prepared you are and the better you do in the interview, the better the recruiter looks in the client's eyes. You are on the same page as the recruiter; view him or her as your ally. Ask for as much pertinent information as you can.

If you're not using a recruiter, it will be more difficult (but not impossible) to obtain all this helpful information. Beyond the plethora of information available online today, do some networking. Start by contacting some of the company's customers. You may find information about current employees beyond the company website (try Google). Go to their business place and gather as much information as you can. Do some mystery shopping and ask questions of as many people as you can. There are websites where people can post "insider info" on companies, but I haven't found them very reliable. Measure negative comments with a grain of salt. A few disgruntled people—constant complainers—can wreak havoc on a company's reputation.

Look for things beyond what you can find on the company website or in the annual report. Ask for the following information:

- Background on the hiring manager (personal and professional). Marital status, children, religion, educational background, hometown, and hobbies.

- Reason for the opening. You want to hear that it's due to promotion or ideally a newly created position. If the previous person was terminated, ask why. If terminated, ask how long was he or she in the position?

- Hot buttons for the company and the hiring manager. What are the most pressing problems they are looking to solve?

- Ideal candidate profile. Which attributes are most important to the hiring manager?

- Key challenges for the job.

- Salary range, including bonus potential and actual payout, benefit information, and perks.
- Company history. When and how did it start? Is it family-owned, private, or publicly traded?

INTERVIEW SNAFUS TO AVOID LIKE THE PLAGUE

As you prepare yourself for the interview (this includes your contact with your recruiter), there are some attitudinal snafus that may derail your interview—even before you have it. These will be a mini-lesson in the concept of contrast, so think of the polar opposite of how to act. These points should go without saying, but you'd be shocked at how many times a candidate commits these blunders:

- Not asking any questions
- Condemning your past employers or bosses
- Being unable to take criticism
- Having poor personal appearance
- Being cynical, lazy, and indecisive
- Being a poor listener, overbearing, and a "know it all"
- Arriving late
- Maintaining poor eye contact
- Being unable to express yourself clearly
- Expressing overemphasis on money

So let's spend some time addressing these situations so you can avoid them.

ATTIRE

Dress codes at companies vary widely these days, but the proper attire for an interview hasn't changed.

As a rule of thumb, always dress your best for the interview. You are probably saying, "C'mon, I know how to dress," but how you dress everyday and how you dress for an interview are two entirely different animals. Even if the company is business casual, men should dress in a conservative suit and tie, and women should wear a conservative suit. Women should look polished but not overdone (minimal jewelry, makeup, and heels that aren't too high).

Navy blue is the best option. Shoes need to be nicely polished and look as if they are brand new. Have your shirts or blouses professionally laundered or choose shirts made of wrinkle-resistant fabric. Have a friend (or a mirror) give you a once-over before you go to the interview. I heard a story of a candidate who waltzed into an interview with toilet paper hanging off the back of his shoe—like a streamer on a float in a parade. He paraded himself out of the job and didn't even realize it.

Your physical impressions get you hired so don't underestimate the power of wearing the proper attire.

VISUALIZATION

This may be the most important way to prepare yourself prior to your interview. If you have been practicing and becoming proficient at meditating (explained earlier), great. If not, you can still visualize. Numerous world-class athletes visualize for success: Tiger Woods, Michael Phelps, and Michael Jordan are a few.

Why is visualization—which has been scientifically proven

to greatly enhance performance and is used widely in athletic competition by the best in the world—rarely used in business? Laziness?

When you learn you have an upcoming interview, spend about 15 minutes before you go to bed visualizing your success. Close your eyes and see yourself in the actual interview. Give yourself sample questions (you can use questions from an upcoming chapter and add your own) and then answer them in your mind. Feel great as you give perfect answers. See the interviewer smile with his or her approval. Feel the connection with the interviewer.

The day of the interview, arrive a half-hour early and find a private place (your car or even the bathroom, if needed) and mentally review all the points you want to make with your interviewer. Mentally give yourself some positive affirmations such as, "I'm going to have a great interview; I'm prepared for any question and confident I'm the right person for the job; this is my dream job."

The practice of visualization is paramount to success in an interview. Meditating—relaxing your mind—just prior to the interview will quell your natural nervousness, allowing you to channel your energy into a productive, positive interview.

When Tiger Woods is preparing to putt, do you think he is thinking anything other than, "I can make the putt"? No! And, usually, he sinks it. The more positive your thoughts are before, during, and after the interview, the more likely you are to nail it.

THREE-SCENES TECHNIQUE

I will provide you with a very powerful application of visualization. Consistent with the message of this book—mystical plus practical—this section will combine meditation with a practical application.

Perform this technique while in the meditative state of alpha. By now, hopefully you are getting more proficient at meditating, and it will come easily to you. If you have not tried to meditate yet, don't worry. This exercise will walk you through it and only take about 15 minutes. Remember, 15 minutes of meditation is the equivalent of two hours of sleep.

With eyes closed, move your eyes as if you were looking slightly upward (about 20 degrees) and picture yourself on your mental screen. Spend about two minutes visualizing yourself right now. See the sights, hear the sounds, feel the feeling all around you. As you begin feeling comfortable, move the image to your right with your eyes and pull the next image of yourself from your left onto your screen in front of you. This will be you in the actual interview. See yourself answering questions with confidence. The questions and answers you are asked are flowing—you have rehearsed and rehearsed (like riding a bicycle). See the interviewer smiling at your answers. Feel the connection. You know you are nailing it. You are well on your way to getting that dream job offer. Hold on to the visualization for about five minutes.

Afterward, again push the screen to the right with your eyes (past) and pull the third visualization from your left (future) onto your center screen (present). This will be you in the job six months from your start date. See yourself doing the job and really enjoying it. Really hone in on the good feeling of being in your blissful dream job—enjoying your work, being recognized for jobs well done, building meaningful relationships with everyone you come in contact with. Be as vivid as you can—the more realistic you can make it, the better. Try to hold this visualization for at least five minutes. When you are ready to finish, feel the gratitude for having your ideal job.

This is one of the most powerful techniques of visualization, and it has been widely used with astounding results.

The stronger and more realistic your thoughts and feelings, the more likely your visualization will manifest into reality.

HOW TO RELAX
BEFORE THE INTERVIEW

We just covered mental preparation prior to an interview. Now, it's time to discuss techniques to relax your body. The application will give you practical results. Remember, you are all energy and vibrate at differing rates from everything else in the universe.

I have read a lot about alternative medicines: chakras, meridians, and acupuncture. If this sounds like Chinese to you, it is! The ancient Chinese, among others, developed amazing techniques to help human beings with their energy flow. Alternative medicine, long disregarded in the U.S. as voodoo medicine, is flourishing today. It's hard to drive for very long and not see a chiropractor's office. There may even be as many chiropractors' offices as McDonald's—now, that's progress.

Rather than give you zillions of things to do and get into the theories behind all this stuff, I'll give you three very simple techniques you can use to overcome nervousness about an upcoming job interview. These will help you release stress and enable your energy to flow optimally—much better than a cup of coffee. All three exercises take only about five minutes total and don't require any heavy lifting. They are called

- K-27s
- Wayne Cook Posture
- Cross Crawl

K-27S

Certain points on your body, when tapped or massaged with your fingers, will positively impact your energy field, sending electro-chemical impulses to your brain and releasing neurotransmitters (feel-good chemicals). By tapping and/or massaging three specific points on your body, you can activate a sequence of responses that will restore you when you are tired, increase your vitality, and even strengthen your immune system amid stress (so you won't get sick before or after the interview).

Figure 1: K-27 Tap

1. Simply place your fingers on your collarbone and slide them inward toward the center and find the bumps where they stop. Drop about an inch beneath these corners and slightly outward to the K-27s (see Figure 1). Most people have a slight indent here that their fingers will drop into.

2. With the fingers of both your hands turned toward your body, cross your hands over one another, with the middle finger of each hand now resting on the opposite K-27 point. Crossing your hands is important because it assists the energy to cross over from the left brain hemisphere to the right side of the body and vice versa—left hemisphere to right side.

3. Tap and/or massage the points firmly while breathing deeply—in through your nose and out through your mouth. Continue for about thirty seconds.

4. After you have tapped/massaged your K-27s, you can boost the effect by hooking the middle finger of one hand in your navel and resting the fingers of your other hand on the K-27 points. With as many fingers as you can hook into your navel, pull upward for two or three deep breaths. You will likely feel a stretch below your belly.

Do this right before your interview. Tapping your K-27s (chakra points) has been proven to help you think more clearly and give you a burst of energy. An interesting side note: Next time you go to a zoo, visit the gorilla cages. If they are active, notice that gorillas will thump their chest and hit their K-27s with their fists before a confrontation with another gorilla. Now, I'm pretty sure that these gorillas didn't read this book, yet they instinctively know how to pump up their energy before a fight—by thumping their K-27s. Smart apes!

WAYNE COOK POSTURE

Named to honor Wayne Cook, a pioneering researcher of bioenergetic force fields, this is a basic technique to literally move stress hormones out of your body. Almost immediately, you will feel better, be able to think more clearly, and see with greater perspective. It can be done in a skirt, but probably best in a semi-private place (the handicapped stall if all else fails). It takes only about two minutes to do the Wayne Cook Posture:

Figure 2: Wayne Cook Posture

1. Sit in a chair with your spine straight. Place your right foot over your left knee. Wrap your left hand around your right ankle and your right hand around the ball of your right foot (see Figure 2).

2. Breathe in slowly through your nose, allowing your breath to lift your body as you breathe in. At the same time, pull your leg toward you, creating a stretch. As you exhale, breathe out of your mouth slowly, and feel your body relax. Repeat this slow breathing and stretching four or five times.

3. Switch to the other foot. Place your left foot over your right knee. Wrap your right hand around your left ankle and your left hand around the ball of your left foot. Use the same breathing.

4. Uncross your legs and place your fingertips together forming a pyramid. Bring your thumbs to rest on your "third eye," just above the bridge of your nose and between your eyes. Breathe slowly in through your nose. Then breathe out through your mouth, allowing your thumbs to separate slowly across your forehead, pulling the skin.

5. Bring your thumbs back to the third eye position. Slowly bring your hands down in front of you, pulling them together into a prayerful position while breathing deeply. Surrender into your own breathing.

Wayne Cook was successful in treating dyslexia and stuttering. This procedure connects the energy circuitry in a manner that allows a smooth flow throughout your body. Stress short-circuits your forebrain (thinking brain). This simple technique will help you communicate clearly and focus well.

CROSS CRAWL

This simple exercise will facilitate the crossover of energy between the brain's right and left hemispheres. You will feel more balanced, think more clearly, improve your coordination (nothing worse than tripping and falling into the interviewer's desk), and harmonize your energies.

Prior to starting the Cross Crawl, tap your K-27s again to ensure that your energies are traveling in their natural direction. The Cross Crawl is very easy to do; it's like marching in place and only takes about a minute:

Figure 3: The Cross Crawl

1. While standing, lift your right arm and left leg simultaneously (see Figure 3).

2. As you let them down, raise your left arm and right leg.

3. Repeat, this time exaggerating the lift of your leg and the swing of your arm across the midline to the opposite side of your body.

4. Continue in this exaggerated march for at least a minute while breathing deeply in through your nose and out through your mouth.

The effectiveness of the Cross Crawl is based primarily on the fact that the left hemisphere of your brain needs to send information to the right side of your body, and vice versa. If energy from the left or right hemisphere is not adequately crossing over to the opposite side of your body, you cannot access and utilize your brain's full capacity or your body's full intelligence. This basic exercise will energize you.

SHOWTIME! THE INTERVIEW

Okay, you are mentally, physically, and emotionally prepared: it's showtime! The big event!

The actual interview itself usually lasts for only an hour. It should help you relax just to realize that one hour will fly by. Bear in mind, there is equal pressure on the interviewer as there is on you, the interviewee.

There is a myth in American business that once a person is promoted to management, he or she becomes magically endowed with all the necessary management skills. Very few people in "management" have been adequately taught to interview (another course that should be offered in schools but isn't). Most junior interviewers just stumble through interviewing and learn from trial and error.

I can still remember conducting my first interview; the term *shaky* is an understatement, but with time and practice, I became proficient in interviewing. You will get a quick sense of the experience level of your interviewer: skilled—savvy in systematic techniques for ferreting out your past and a good evaluator of your skills from effective Q&As; or bumbling—he or she may even have trouble phrasing questions adequately. Both are equally challenging when it comes to winning an offer. The advice you will receive will help you with all types of interviewers.

Beyond the all-important first impression, there are four sections to the interview. The more prepared you are for each section, the more likely the interview will produce an offer. The following are the four major sections of the interview:

- The introduction
- Your background
- Information about the company
- Closing (discussed in detail in chapter 7)

THE INTRODUCTION

If you feel a little nervous, congratulate yourself, you are a human being. You are, after all, interviewing for your ideal job. The more you are able to channel your nervous energy into an amazing performance, the more likely you are to receive an offer. Tell yourself you're ready and take some relaxing deep breaths. The introduction is the easy part.

A firm handshake while smiling and smoothly introducing yourself is the most important element toward making a strong first impression. Many interviewers say, "I make my mind up about a candidate in the first five seconds." Do not underestimate this vital step. If your nerves have given you a clammy, wet hand, wipe it off right before the handshake. If your hand is cold, warm it up—run hot water in the bathroom if necessary. The firm handshake has to leave a favorable impression.

After the initial greeting, follow the interviewer's lead on where to sit and remember to keep your posture upright. Your posture should reflect confidence and professionalism—a comfortable readiness.

Allow the interviewer to "break the ice," usually by picking a light topic: the weather, the surroundings, a current event. Again, follow the interviewer's lead and ease into the interview with grace.

How well you handle this first five minutes usually determines whether or not the interviewer feels comfortable with you (and vice versa). You'll know when the introduction section is over because the interviewer will transition from small talk to an introductory question.

YOUR BACKGROUND

An astute interviewer will usually try to get you to talk about 80 percent of the time by asking open-ended questions like these:

- *Tell me about yourself?*
- *What brings you here today?*
- *First, I'd like you to walk me through your background.*

I will give you great sample answers to these open-ended questions and many others in the next chapter.

The Two Most Important Questions

Keep in mind, there is pressure on the interviewer. It is a difficult task to get to know you in the confines of an hour or less. There are two critical questions in the back of the interviewer's mind:

- *Why do you want to leave your current company?*
- *Why do you want to work for us?*

The *Why do you want to leave your current company?* question is a potential landmine. Don't step on the landmine. The answer needs to be brief and well-prepared. Less is more here. Many interviewees open up Pandora's Box at this point, thinking that brutal honesty is what's needed now—as a way to bond with the interviewer. Don't let your guard down.

The interviewer actually doesn't want to hear about all the evil things your boss has done to you in the past, or all the broken promises, or all the times you were overlooked for a promotion, or screwed out of a bonus, or how bad the training is, or how horrible the culture is. In fact, usually, the interviewer is wincing inside as this question is asked, hoping you don't commit interview suicide by stepping on that landmine.

So, what's the best answer? If you are using an executive search firm, tell the interviewer you weren't looking, that things have been going well, and that the recruiter kept persisting and, after looking at the opportunity, you agreed it would be a great job and company. Perfect. You have remained positive, upbeat, and even confident, without smearing your previous company.

If the company was not using a search firm, use the "I wasn't really looking—I'm happy here, but this opportunity seemed like a dream job. I've always wanted to work for this company, and customer X and Y and Z have spoken highly about your company."

Another possible answer is, "Well as you've probably seen in *The Wall Street Journal,* our company is being divested and though I have enjoyed my work, there is uncertainty about our future." The interviewer will usually nod in agreement even if he or she doesn't read *The Wall Street Journal*—just being able to quote the business bible is impressive and also shows you know how to read.

The quicker you get to the next question, *Why do you want to work for us?* the better. In this important step, you win the job or lose it. In an interview, it's usually not the most qualified person—on paper—who gets the job; it's the person who goes in to get a job versus merely to have a job interview.

That deserves repeating: it's the person who goes in to get a job who wins the offer; merely showing up for an interview doesn't cut it. Enthusiasm toward the company, the job, and the opportunity can make all the difference in the world.

Prepare your answer. It needs to be brief, positive, genuine, and enthusiastic. Say, "I have always wanted to work for this company and this job seems ideal for my background." Tell the interviewer what you can bring to the table by using examples of your experiences.

Brag Book

The brag book is a very important item to bring to the interview. Many times, an interviewer will ask you to describe your accomplishments, successes, desirable personality traits, and so on. It is very effective to have this information in print form as a leave-behind and as a talking point during the interview. Your brag book should contain this information:

- A clean cotton-bound copy of your résumé
- Performance appraisals

- Examples of your work, particularly ones that were successful and would be important to the interviewer
- Letters of recommendation
- Copies of awards you have won

Place this information in a binder or folder and hand it to the interviewer as quickly as possible. A brag book gives the impression that you are professional, want the job badly enough to take the time to put it together, and takes the BS factor out of verbal-only answers.

What is the BS factor? Anyone can BS their way through an interview, but a written leave-behind is much more believable. It's one thing to say, "I'm persistent, a team player, and a high achiever," and an entirely different—and more effective technique—to show it with what bosses actually wrote about you and with examples of your work. A sample of your work shows the work and is instantly impressive and believable.

Finally, your brag book is a way to differentiate yourself from the others after the interviews have ended. The interviewer is likely to read through it after your one-hour interview has ended. In essence, you are able to sell yourself even after you have gone; your brag book can sway the decision your way without your having to say a word; it's all been said by those who have observed your work.

In addition, the brag book makes an interviewer less apt to feel the need to obtain references on you—something that can backfire if the wrong person is contacted—unbeknownst to you (we all have a few enemies; it's no coincidence that the word *enemy* is similar to *envy*).

Remember, it's not always the most qualified person for the job who gets the job. The person who wants the job the most, gets the job. The brag book shows you want the job.

INFORMATION ABOUT THE COMPANY

By now, you have either won the job—which you will feel—or the interviewer has kept his or her nonverbal signals hidden. This is the homestretch. A little previous preparation and improvisation will keep the momentum building in your favor.

Usually the interviewer will shift into asking you, "Do you have any questions for me?" An enthusiastic yes is required; answering no can drop you out of the running. Prepare a list of questions for this interaction. It is very common to blank out at this point, so having a notebook/sheet of paper right there in front of you will help greatly.

Try to prioritize your questions using the "put yourself in the interviewer's shoes" mode. This is your opportunity to shine (pun intended)—showing you have done your research. You should ask "kiss up" questions—incorporating genuine positives about the company into your questions. For example:

- *Everyone I've talked to—customers, competitors, and even former employees—say that your company is a great place to work. What do you think makes it tick?*

- *Your financial results have been impressive and at the top of the industry. Where do you think this company will be in five years?*

- *I've been very impressed with your latest product/service. What do you think has been your company's greatest achievement?*

The trick with these questions is to connect with your interviewer's perspective. This is imperative. Avoid asking critical questions (the Nuremberg approach) that put the interviewer on the defensive. Do not ask any negative questions about the results or the culture of the company. Verboten: if the company is coming off a lousy year, don't turn on the bright lights and pick a scab. Ask the negative questions *after* you receive the offer. Conversely, if you can get the interviewer to feel good about your questions, you have probably sealed the deal at this point.

8

Tell Me about Yourself

At some point, the interviewer takes over and starts asking you a whole litany of questions. Many interviewers bring prepared questions. Several undisciplined candidates experience fear at this phase of the interview. Fear is rooted in lack of confidence in the future. Think about it. Fear is nothing more than an irrational lack of focus on the present.

It is important for you to be confident, focused, and in the present moment, for the interview. The purpose of this section is to give you the confidence that you can answer any question. The following are sample interview questions, taken from actual interviews—with examples of good answers. Feel free to use these exact phrases if they feel natural to you, but remember to customize your answers to highlight your individual strengths and showcase your blissful personality.

Interviewing is an art, a skill that requires the 3 P's: practice, practice, practice. Use these interview questions as a guide to help you practice. You cannot overprepare for an interview. Practice with someone asking these questions, then try reading each question and answering into a mirror. Finally, meditate and visualize the interview, your answers, and the interviewer smiling as he or she offers you the job.

Q:
Tell me about yourself.

This is possibly the most common interview question. First, ask a qualifier: "Are you interested in my business or personal life?" Then, put yourself in the interviewer's shoes for your answer. Be prepared for "both" as the answer. Intersperse as many of the following traits as you can into your answer:

Personal Traits

- **Enthusiastic:** Many interviewers expect you to entertain them. The more engaged you are with genuine energy and enthusiasm, the more likely you are to win the job offer. Your enthusiasm is contagious.

- **Positive:** You see the glass as full every time. There is always upside potential.

- **Initiative:** You set very lofty goals for yourself (have examples in mind) and strive to accomplish your goals through action.

- **Determined:** Paint yourself as a winner despite all obstacles and make it clear that you embrace new challenges.

- **Confident:** There's a fine line between seeming *cocky* and being *confident*. I'd like you to break out the brag book here with some previous performance appraisals and highlight your positive traits through what your previous supervisors wrote about you.

- **Concise thinker:** Do not let yourself ramble on during this or any other answer.

- **Communicator:** Your ability to verbalize your thoughts and write effective e-mails and proposals are important to any company.

Business Traits

- **Integrity:** The cornerstone to any effective relationship. You always treat decisions as if you owned the company yourself. You follow the motto: "Do what's right."
- **Efficient:** By setting your goals and efficiently managing your time, you get the job done right—and quickly.
- **Reliable:** You are always counted on, and trusted, to get any task done and done right.
- **Analytical:** You make educated decisions based on facts and weigh the pros and cons carefully.
- **Proud:** You do only work that makes you proud and again—referring to your brag book/performance appraisal(s)—that makes your supervisors proud.
- **Personable:** You are a good listener, but can verbalize your thoughts in a concise, cohesive manner to best communicate any subject.
- **Problem solving:** You are a problem solver who can run the business.

Try to be concise in your answer and tailor it to the needs of the position and the company. Practice your response as often as you can.

Q:
What are your three greatest strengths and three greatest weaknesses?

This is a very common interview question. The first part is a slam dunk; the second is a potential landmine unless you are careful. For strengths, keep in mind that every company needs people who can do three things well: (1) earn revenue, (2) save money, and (3) save time. Plug this in, interspersed with some business traits and make the interviewer smile.

For weaknesses, don't ingest truth serum and tell of your paranoid fantasy to kill your current boss. Avoid admitting to character flaws like the plague. I prefer a "weakness" to be skill-related and past tense: "I wasn't astute with PowerPoint when I first started, but I read a great book, practiced, and became very proficient; now I train others in PowerPoint presentations."

You are admitting to something that everyone had trouble with at first. You are not born with computer software skills, so this is not a damaging answer; furthermore, you can show that you are a quick study, able to learn it and then teach it. Any time you can demonstrate how you overcame a weakness, all the better.

Another good "weakness" example is to give a general answer in which you can plug perceived strengths: "I am passionate about my work and always give each task my all. So, when sometimes I see others loafing, I can get frustrated. I have improved by always trying to demonstrate a positive attitude and hope it will catch on," or "I set lofty goals for myself and am sometimes too demanding of myself."

Again, you have another chance to mention that you are a goal-setter who raises the bar very high. Not a bad weakness. The trick with discussing your weaknesses is to avoid the landmine answer. Turn your weakness into an actual strength with a throw-away, past-tense skill that you have now learned.

Q:
What keeps you up at night?

Another landmine that you cannot step on. This is another way of asking for weaknesses. As you begin to feel more and more comfortable with the interviewer, there is a tendency to let your guard down. Don't! The answer is: "Aside from the occasional nightmare about interviewing, I work so hard that I rarely have a difficult time sleeping. I believe in proper time management and recharging my batteries with sound sleep. I'm no good to anyone if I'm tired."

Q:
Tell me how you progressed through your last company.

A good question particularly if he or she is looking for a promotable candidate. Here you can intersperse more about your personal and business traits. Be very complimentary of the company you work for: "The training was superb" or "I was fortunate to have had some great mentors who really helped me." It will be hard not to ramble a little, but focus on the promotions by title as a result of dedicated hard work and outstanding accomplishments with downright genius. If you haven't been formally promoted, mention a few new challenges you've faced and how you've overcome them.

Q:
How would your boss describe you?

You can immediately point to the brag book packet you handed over during the interview, which contained a fresh copy of your résumé, previous performance appraisals, examples of your work, and letters of recommendation. This show-and-tell gives you greater credibility in the eyes of the interviewer. It can be very powerful to point out that your boss wrote, "Joe Schmoe is a top performer, dedicated, takes tremendous pride in his work, and sets demanding goals for himself. I have learned from him."

Q:
How would your spouse describe you?

This one can be tricky if you are going through a bitter divorce. Even if you are—and it's none of the interviewer's business—the answer is always an upbeat, positive response: "Loving, generous, supportive, inspirational, fun to be around, and a great role-model for our kids."

Q:
If you could be a color, which one would you be?

I was actually asked this question by an impressive, Ivy-League–educated, African-American female in a high-powered job interview. Talk about a landmine question for a Caucasian male! If I answered "black," I would have been seen as kissing up to her, and disingenuous; if I answered "white," I would seem like a member of the Klan.

I smiled and answered: "The rainbow." She smiled, looked interested and asked, "Why?" I replied, "There are four basic personality types in individuals, and I pride myself on trying to recognize and adapt to each one, depending on the situation. Sometimes I need to be red; sometimes green; sometimes black and white; sometimes even pink."

She laughed and actually said, "Great answer!"

(For this question, there are a rainbow of ways to answer—and back up with a colorful example.)

Q:
If you could be an animal, which one would you be?

I was asked this as the follow up to the color question. My instinct told me to avoid saying panther and polar bear—no benefit in messing up my previous answer with the black and white thing. Also, shark, snake, and turtle were landmine replies.

I answered, "Jaguar." She looked intrigued, smiled, and asked, "Why?"

I replied, "The jaguar is very versatile—able to patiently wait for its prey for hours on end if needed and can pounce with lightning speed and grace. Plus, it's a cool car!"

She smiled and said, "Great answer" for the second time as she reached into her purse to pull out her car keys with the Jaguar emblem on it (I got the job offer).

(Again, there are many ways to answer this question, none of them wrong—the key is to have a positive rationale for your choice.)

Q:
How long would you stay with our company?

This is a good question to get asked; it is a "buy" signal, implying he or she is thinking of offering you a job. This one is tricky though—*is he or she concerned that I would leave after a short while?*

Don't take the bait. Put the hot potato back in the interviewer's lap with: "I would hope to have a great career with this company. I respond well to direction and am always looking to learn. I define success as being ready when an opportunity arises. How long do you think I'd be challenged here?" Back in his or her lap. Touché!

Q:
Describe how you do a major project.

This is a perfect opportunity to demonstrate that you are a business manager who can identify and solve problems: "I believe in effective strategic planning that involves both forward thinking (in other words, what resources will I need?) and backward thinking (for example, if the deadline is the end of the quarter, what steps need to be made and at what time to achieve a successful outcome?)."

Q:
How do you handle stress?

This is tricky; the interviewer implies you get stressed out. Does the interviewer mean personal stress or business stress inherent to business cycles?

The best way to answer this is to deflect it, "I avoid stress by careful time management. There are only so many hours in a given day, so I try to maximize my time by setting effective goals. On the personal side, I exercise regularly, eat right, and get adequate sleep—I think this alleviates stress."

Q:
What would you do during your first ninety days on the job?

Fair question in the interviewer's mind but unfair to the interviewee. The interviewer cannot expect you to know the intricacies of the position and the company, so you can be general here.

After responding with some generalities, I like to send this one back to the interviewer. "I believe in setting my goals in line with the company's near-term objectives, which I would expect to receive right away. Then I would prioritize my time relative to achieving those goals. What are the company's most pressing needs right now and do you offer a standard training program?"

Q:
Are you open to relocation?

Hopefully, prior to the interview, you were able to find out where the position is located—out of your home office (as is becoming more accepted), in a branch office, or inside the corporate headquarters. If unsure, say, "It's my understanding that this job would be out of my home office. Is that right?"

If the answer is a "yes but," find out where the hiring manager wants you located and answer accordingly. Keep in mind, your objective in the interview is to get the job offer first; then you can decide. If, unbeknownst to you, they want to move you to Nowheresville, Kentucky, you can always say no.

Don't take yourself out of the running now based on location. If the question is, "Would you move for a promotion?" the answer is, "I would consider relocation for the right opportunity to grow with the company." Even if your sick, live-in, mother-in-law is in your basement and your spouse would crucify you for even considering relocation, don't step on the landmine by answering no.

After you are with a company and have proven yourself to be a valuable employee, many times there is flexibility on location. Make sure your answer keeps you in the running.

Q:
What experience do you have for this job?

This is a key question in the back of the mind of the interviewer but unfortunately, without proper background information, you should not answer blindly. It is proper to ask a qualifier such as, "What are some of the problems facing the company currently, and what projects will I be involved in?" Only by asking this qualifier will you identify the priorities of your future boss.

The interviewer will think favorably of your thought process with this qualifier. The interviewer's answer will give you enough ammo so you can adequately answer the question. Use your brag book if you can show examples of your having accomplished like tasks and solving similar problems. The more you show yourself as a problem-solver who can run the business, the better.

Q:
What do you like and dislike about your current job?

This is what I call the "wince question"—the interviewer winces just after asking it, hoping you don't step on a landmine by blurting out a negative answer.

This takes you back to, "Why do you want to leave your current company?" Don't take the bait. Even if your current company is a torture chamber, don't tell the interviewer. He or she is actually looking for you to give a positive response and not rant and rave about your current job and company.

Focus on the positives. Say, "As you know, I wasn't looking and am doing well in my current job. I love the training and the culture.

Our products and services are superb. My boss is supportive and a great teacher. But my company is being sold, so I'm concerned about future security. Regardless of my company's security, both this opportunity and your company seem ideal to me."

If your company is not being sold (even though every publically traded company technically is up for sale), you can always say, "The company is small and there isn't much room for me to grow." If the reverse is true, say, "I'm looking for a smaller company where I can make a big difference."

Be upbeat about all your experiences and shift gears to show how applicable your training is to the job for which you are interviewing. It may be a good time to point to your brag book if you have an example of applicable work that was exemplary. Use the comment, "As you know, I wasn't actively looking . . . but, the more I looked into this company and this position, the more interested I became."

The interviewer by now has probably given you some information about what's important. Hit 'em with his or her own "hot buttons" here.

Q:
What parts of your job do you consider most important?

Under the pressure of an interview, many candidates immediately think of the opposite, conjuring up all the things they hate about their current job. There's also a tendency to dive into minutiae and rattle off meaningless tasks as they pop in your head. Caution: exercise care. Opening any can of worms can derail your progress and end the interview fast.

Think "big picture" in your answer and intersperse positive

character traits. Remember, you want to paint yourself as someone who is a business manager who can run the business. Try, "My ability to manage my time wisely. First, I set daily goals, prioritizing them in order of importance, and then attack them until completion—while avoiding distractions." Be prepared to list an example of an impressive accomplishment (This is a great time to point to your brag book).

Q:
How do you feel about working overtime?

Now's not the time to tell the interviewer how you cannot work any extra hours because you are training for the Iron Man Triathlon and have a sick parent and see a shrink five times per week for your paranoid fantasy about killing your boss. The best answer is, "Though I pride myself on time-management and prioritization skills, I realize that extra time is sometimes needed."

Q:
What are you hoping to gain from this job?

Be leery of mentioning any aspects of your background where you may lack experience. This is not the time to tell the hiring manager how he or she can help you build your résumé. Make sure you know the challenges of the job that are important to the interviewer (remember, put yourself in his or her shoes). If not, answer in vague terms and sneak in a qualifier, "I'm hoping to utilize my training and experience to help the company achieve its goals. What are your most pressing needs during my first year?" Did you notice how I slipped in the assumed close—that I had the job already—with "during my first year"? The interviewer's reply will reveal a treasure trove of information. Listen carefully, take notes, then shoot back examples of how you accomplished like tasks.

Point to the brag book if you can. Unload some more ideal personal and business traits here. Convince the interviewer that you can step right in and tackle the challenges immediately. The more the interviewer has confidence that you can do it, the more likely you will obtain the offer.

Q:

Your experience is not in our industry. Do you think you can succeed in a different industry?

This one is comical in a way. Every employer feels that what they do is the most complicated and difficult thing imaginable. The truth of the matter is, everything can be learned with proper fundamentals. Emphasize those of your fundamentals that are universally desired. Draw from your ideal personal and business traits.

If this issue really were a knockout punch for your candidacy, then you wouldn't be given an interview in the first place. Don't cower; display confidence that you are a quick study with a demonstrated track record of success.

Q:

Have you ever been terminated from your job?

If you haven't, this is an easy answer, "No, and I don't plan on it happening anytime soon!"

This is a very tricky response if you have. It's really none of the interviewer's business anyway, but an unqualified yes opens up

Pandora's Box, taking up the better part of the valuable and limited remaining interview time.

In my career, every company I joined either sold outright or the division I was in was put on the chopping blocks. The 1980s might have produced some cool music—and hair bands—but in business, it was nearly impossible to avoid going through corporate mergers and acquisitions, downsizings, rightsizings, cutbacks, layoffs, workforce reductions, bankruptcies, and closings (dot-com people please stand up). If anything, the period produced more creative ways for employers to say, "You're fired!"

If you were part of a job loss due to a dot-bomb not making it, it's not going to do you any harm to be "let go." Same with acquisitions (the acquirer is usually the conqueror). But if you were terminated for cause or any other performance reason, and there is a gap on your résumé, be prepared with a concise, convincing answer like, "While at Company XYZ, as you may know, we went through a number of department closings and downsizings. The department I was in was affected, and I was offered an early-retirement package. I took it and spent the time exploring all my options and patiently looking for the right job. The generous financial package allowed me to be patient so I didn't have to jump at the first offer that I received."

End by flipping it back in the interviewer's lap with, "What is the likelihood of a downsizing in this company?"

If you were fired with cause—short of criminal activity—it will be very difficult for a potential employer to obtain this information during a reference check. Ask your previous employer what they reveal during a reference check. Most companies have very strict policies (usually prompted by court cases) about giving only the previous employee's name, dates of employment, and job title(s). I'm not saying you should lie, but you should think long and hard about your answer—and avoid interview suicide.

Q:
Describe a challenging time when others relied on you to interpret information for them.

The interviewer is looking for your ability to communicate in an understandable way. Avoid merely restating what was communicated with little adaptation around the recipient's needs.

A possible answer is, "I was a member of a seven-person, multi-functional task force. Our challenge was to come up with a solution for a problem we were having on one of our production lines. There was some technical data that seemed like ancient hieroglyphics to everyone, but I was able to disseminate it into a usable, recommended solution. I pride myself on using all of the information available, and making it practical—in understandable language."

Q:
Describe your most effective speech.

If you have ever had any training in speech and communication, interject it now; it shows you are a professional who is properly trained.

I attended Executive Techniques, a two-day training seminar during which each participant critiqued the other presentations. It provided very useful feedback and helped me improve my presentation skills immensely.

Many schools offer courses in public speaking; mention your experience if you can. If you haven't had any professional training or courses, describe your planning and mastery of the subject ahead of time, and use of visuals (PowerPoint knowledge is a benefit to most employers) and your overall presentation techniques.

Avoid talking about your phobia of public speaking and the fact that you have a persistent incontinence problem when you are put on the spot in front of a group of people.

Q:

Tell me about a time when you had to communicate under difficult circumstances.

This is similar to the "interpret information" question just discussed—only this one focuses on your communication skills.

Speak to your preparation and mastery of the content and that you had a good understanding of the problem from carefully listening. The perception of a presentation is that it is 90 percent talking, but you believe that the most effective communication stems from 90 percent listening and 10 percent talking. After you fully understood the problem, you focused on the problem and did not personalize it (in other words, you didn't let egos get in the way). Say that your direct answer, which focused on the solution, was well-received and appreciated. Don't stray into any negative feelings you may have had—focus on how you attacked the problem with the right solution by using all of the available information.

Q:

Careful listening and effective communication go hand in hand. Tell me about a specific time when your skill in listening helped you communicate better.

This is the interviewer's way of saying, "Okay, I liked that answer, but I'm going to ask the same question in a slightly different way—let's see what you've got. Give me another example?"

This is a clever way of ferreting out whether you were full of BS or have some substance to your answers. Point to your brag book. Chances are your previous performance appraisals (the good ones that is) provide an opening for you to speak about your ability to solve a problem. Perhaps a meeting where you offered a solution to a problem that had the rest of the table stumped. Of course you did this through your listening skills and you responded in a way that related to the other person's needs in a clear, concise manner. And end with how well received your response was.

Q:

Tell me about the most complex information you ever had to read and how did you comprehend it. Be specific.

I always like the "be specific." Translated, it means, "Don't BS me with some flowery general answer!"

We all have read stuff that gave us an instant headache (for me, it's the instruction manual that is stuffed in the box of any unassembled thing). Since the interviewer wanted "specific" (no BS), pick some technical information or research that may be applicable to the company with whom you are interviewing. Answer that you pride yourself on being able to assimilate complex technical information into a brief presentation. We all are inundated with information, so the ability to make seemingly complex information easy to understand is a very desirable trait.

Q:

This job will require you to spend a large amount of time writing. Tell me about your writing experiences that you think will contribute to your ability to do this job well.

Being an English major at Boston College, I loved this question. I would always intersperse my Technical Writing course—in which I earned an "A"—as a very helpful guide in effective written communication.

If you don't have any training in writing, answer that the most effective written communication is clear, concise, with a purpose, and, most importantly, a solution. If you have ever had anything published, bring it in your brag book and do a little show-and-tell.

Q:

You have described yourself as a problem-solver who can run the business. Give me an example.

This is a great way to demonstrate your desirable skills. Emphasize that you always use a disciplined process to define the problem, identify the root cause(s), evaluate data from a variety of sources, generate alternative solution, and choose the best solution.

Have examples and, again, if any are in the brag book, pull 'em out. The most believable answers are the ones the interviewer can wrap his or her hands around—or better yet, see.

Q:
*Tell me about your business judgment
and decision-making skills.*

They are looking for your ability to identify problems or opportunities and recognize symptoms, causes, and alternative solutions. Also, your ability to make timely, sound decisions even under conditions of risk and uncertainty.

You are an experienced business manager who can run the business. If you have any relevant professional training, mention it. I took a fantastic two-day seminar by Kepner-Tregoe on Problem-Solving and Decision Making, held at Harvard University. Just to mention Harvard in an interview impresses your audience (except to a Boston College guy). The course taught an effective way to determine key needs and wants and a system of ranking them in priority and then attacking the problem based on facts not on emotion.

If you don't have the time for a two-day seminar, give an example of a solution you proposed to help solve a pressing company problem.

Q:
*One of the things I love about the company is
that we are feedback-rich and team-based.
Describe an experience that would help you
thrive in this environment.*

The interviewer is looking for relationship management skills, communication, attention to detail, planning/prioritizing/goal setting, leadership, flexibility, influence, and persuasion.

Preface your answer with, "I'm glad to hear that. My current company sounds similar," and then give your example. End with, "I thrive in an environment where constructive feedback is welcomed."

Q:
Describe your leadership skills.

Demonstrate your ability to convince others to express desirable behavior and to take specific action. You pride yourself on leading by example. Integrate one or more of the following into your answer: "being able to effectively persuade, motivate, lead, empower others, negotiate, act positively, create opportunities, and influence others."

Q:
I asked you earlier about your written communication skills, but tell me about your overall communication skills.

It is clever when the interviewer pulls a Detective Columbo and sheepishly asks a question again—in a slightly different way. The interviewer is likely looking for consistency in your answer and a more general assessment of your skills in this important competency.

Answer that you pride yourself on your ability to communicate effectively in a variety of settings: one-on-one, group, and in front of a large audience. In the one-on-one and small group settings, you pride yourself on your listening skills (remember the 90 percent listening example given in one of your previous answers), your written and verbal communication skills, plus your training and experience in presenting, speaking, consulting, and updating.

Q:
*Tell me how you coach
and develop talent.*

This is another way of asking how you manage people with a twist.

You always strive for positive reinforcement in your coaching with direct and timely feedback. You have a commitment to learning and treat each person how you would want to be treated (good old Golden Rule). Close with examples of people you have hired, trained, and promoted to greater responsibilities—and how great it made you feel.

Q:
*Give me an example of your
interpersonal skill level
and how you applied it to overcome
a difficult situation.*

You want to use an example in which you illustrate your ability to interact with others in ways that build and maintain cooperative working relationships. You handle difficult situations using the same fundamentals as seemingly easy situations, focusing on relationship building, using a pleasant, nonthreatening demeanor and tone, with respect and tact, empathy, and above all, high integrity and ethical standards.

Q:

You will be working as a team quite often in this role, many times with a variety of functions. How do you view teamwork?

If you have examples—perhaps in your brag book, or listed on your résumé (a good idea)—use them right away. You believe in collaborative effort in order to obtain the greatest results. Be prepared to speak of some multifunctional teams you have served on, especially if you led the team.

Stress that you encouraged full participation of every team member (demonstrating a value of differences) and ultimately, through conflict resolution techniques, your teams always came up with creative, effective, and timely solutions to a wide range of tasks/problems.

Q:

You mentioned "initiative" earlier. Tell me about how you used initiative and creativity to solve a problem.

Try, "I pride myself on heading a problem off at the pass—before it affects business. A pro-active approach always saves the company money and increases productivity. There is always more than one alternative to solve a problem. I use creativity in my decision making and problem-solving techniques."

With my training seminar experience, when I was asked this question, I was able to answer, "My Kepner-Tregoe course taught me to list key wants and needs and then to prioritize them. This disciplined approach allowed me to creatively consider all alternatives before arriving at a decision that is fact-based and timely." If you didn't enroll in a K-T seminar, you can still use the fundamentals that I mentioned.

Q:
I like your creativity and it sounds as if you have a strong analytical side. Describe it.

Show that you summarize information well to identify and highlight key elements, patterns, results, or relationships. Have examples of using a variety of analytical techniques to organize data. Then say you always ask a series of questions that are designed to surface additional and new information about the problem—attacking all problems from all angles—as if in 3D.

Also mention that you draw on past experience with similar situations to recognize patterns of causality. From there, you quickly separate relevant from irrelevant facts and then develop and test several hypotheses about the source of the problem.

Q:
What is your greatest accomplishment?

Does the interviewer mean personal or business? Ask the qualifier and if the answer is "both," great; if it is "pick one over the other in rank," go with business—maybe a major promotion that was a culmination of all of your hard work, accomplishments, and dedication.

Stay clear of mentioning the "birth of my first child" answer in a business interview; though it may be true—and probably should be—keep in mind that you are interviewing for a professional job.

Q:
Do you have any questions?

An important question and you always have questions. Responding, "No, I think we covered it all," gets you the boot. This is also the interviewer's not-so-subtle way of drawing the interview to a close.

This one is your last chance to leave a favorable impression. Come prepared with a notepad with at least five good questions that demonstrate your research on the company. I like the kiss-up questions here: "With the impressive results the company has had in the last five years, where do you see the company in five years?" or "I've heard some wonderful things about your company. How do you think your competitors feel about your company?" or "Customer XYZ said great things about your company and your high-quality service levels, how do other customers view you?"

After the brown-nose questions, ask, "What key skills and attributes are most needed to succeed in this job?" After the interviewer gives you the answer, plug in some examples of demonstrated success you have in each of these areas.

Q:
Rate yourself on a scale of 1 to 10 on how weird you are.

This question opens the door to an important element in any interpersonal interaction—humor. This question explores whether you take yourself too seriously. Don't make the mistake of saying, "I'm not weird at all." Hiring managers are looking for unique individuals and not robots so, assuming the position you're interviewing for requires some analytics (and most do), I like a levity answer, "I'm a 4.78149327."

Q:
What would you do if you won the lottery?

I was asked this question after I already thought I had the offer in the bag. I said, "Pay off all my debt, invest wisely to provide for me and my family for the rest of our lives, and truly enjoy this job without financial concerns." The interviewer smirked as she shot back, "Boring."

I retorted, "What would you do?"

She said, "I'd quit, buy a big house in Jamaica, and sit on the beach every day."

I took a calculated risk with my reply, "With all of your education and accomplishments, you'd be bored in two weeks. You're a high achiever and sitting on a beach all the time would drive you nutty." She laughed (good sign) and said, "True, but I'd take a nice long vacation." I nailed the offer.

Q:
Sell me this pen.

This is a common interview question for a variety of sales jobs, especially entry level. It's a test of your ability to open, persuade, then close. The interviewer is looking for your ability to uncover the customer's needs and wants, to select key features of the product, and to sell the benefits of these features. The benefits should meet the customer's needs and make the sale. A basic rule of selling is to sell the benefits the customer will gain from the product rather than the list of features the product has. Don't make the mistake of getting caught up in minutia—babbling about all the features—before you know what the customer's hot buttons are. Ask, "What's important to you when selecting a pen?" Then listen carefully. After you have enough pertinent information, list the relevant benefits and always ask for the order.

TESTING

Many companies require mental and emotional testing of potential employees as a prerequisite to employment. Don't worry—there's not much you can do in the form of preparation, other than getting a good night's rest and having a good mindset.

I have seen companies employ a litany of tests: IQ, personality, emotional, psychological, business, math, and even testing following training (especially in pharmaceutical companies). The way I look at these tests is that if it's meant to be, it will be. Don't give yourself an ulcer over any pre-employment testing. It's not as daunting as it may seem.

Having said that, there is a strategy to employ when answering personality and emotional test questions: Be consistent.

Often you will be asked the same question three different times in three different ways. Inconsistency in your answers is usually a knock-out punch. The best advice is to consistently answer with your "business mind"—thinking about what they are looking for.

So if a company is looking for a salesperson, don't say you're timid (you'd be surprised at how many times this has happened); for a marketing manager, don't say you lack creativity; for a production position, don't say you have a difficult time with continuous tasks.

Put yourself in their shoes and answer according to the required tasks and desired traits for the position you are seeking.

SAVVY INTERVIEW TECHNIQUES

One of my largest clients employed an interesting and demanding screening process. After the first interview with the hiring manager, they brought the candidate in to their headquarters for "finals." At finals, they had eight managers in different functions grill the candidate on eight different topics and then grade the performance. (I called it the "grill & grade.")

These were the eight topics (and some clarification of their meaning):

1. Cultural fit (background, interests, and work ethic)

2. Teamwork (the ability to share due credit with coworkers, display enthusiasm, and promote a friendly group environment; team spirit)

3. Planning/prioritizing/goal setting (organizational and time management skills)

4. Relationship management (interpersonal skills and the ability to work with a wide range of personality types)

5. Communication (clear thinker with strong verbal and written communication skills)

6. Leadership (the ability to assume a role of authority, advocate new insights, even when risk is involved; a role model)

7. Flexibility (the ability to adapt to a wide range of demands and an evolving work environment)

8. Influence and persuasion (the ability to clearly verbalize a position and inspire improvement)

After these eight interviews, the candidate would meet with the president and CEO who would ask the candidate to interview him (we'll discuss this in a moment).

And after a full day of interviews, the candidate would fly to a different city to take an IQ test, personality test, and sit face-to-face with a psychiatrist who would then personally shrink test the poor slob for an hour, with questions like, "Which parent do you like the least?" Yikes! Please don't tell my mom and dad my choice, doc. He actually made one of my finalists cry with his imposing questions (she didn't get the job).

Don't fret if you are faced with a daunting selection process; be grateful that the company is so selective and have confidence in your abilities. And back to my original advice: prepare. You can imagine the difference in your "grade" if you are aware of what they are looking for ahead of time (such as their eight topics of importance) versus going in blind. Be prepared.

WHEN THE INTERVIEWER ASKS YOU TO INTERVIEW HIM OR HER

This happens frequently, particularly with savvy interviewers; they can measure you by the questions you ask them. If you are prepared—and you are—this is an easy interview.

If the person is a senior manager (especially a CEO), ask strategic questions such as, *Where do you see this company in five years?* Additional questions to ask:

- *Why did you join the company?*
- *What has changed since you joined?*
- *What would you like to change?*
- *Why is the position open?*
- *What strategic advantages does your company have over your competitors?*
- *How do your customers view you?*

- *What are the first three priorities you would like to see accomplished by the person chosen to fill this position?*
- *Where does this position fit into the scheme of things?*
- *What does this company value the most and how do you think my work for you will further these values?*
- *Where do you see me in five years with this company?*
- *What's the makeup of the team in terms of experience? Will I be a mentor or will I be mentored or both?*
- *What's the most important thing I can do for this company?*
- *When top performers leave the company, why do they leave and where do they usually go?*

By now, you've answered the questions and earned an "A" grade, taken the tests and survived. Now, it's time to get the offer. It's closing time.

CLOSING

Usually, the interviewer will indicate that time is up.

Always ask for the job before leaving! It is a final and important opportunity to grab the job. The best "closes" are brief, direct, and spoken with confidence.

A great sample closing is this: *Do you have any concerns about my ability to do this job or any subsequent jobs with this company in the future?* If the answer is no, then reply, *When can I start?* If yes, find out what the concern is and then overcome the objection with examples of your work.

More astute interviewers may say yes just to test your mettle and see how you behave under pressure—one final time. Be confident and direct in your answer and ask for the job one last time.

WHAT DO THEY SAY ABOUT YOU AFTER YOU LEAVE?

You've created a killer résumé, networked yourself like a Tasmanian Devil, and prepared, prepared, and prepared for the interview. Two people grilled you for over an hour. What happens when you leave?

The reality is that many interviewers hire in their own likeness. This includes hometown, religious upbringing, political affiliation, gender, ethnicity, education, and image. This doesn't mean you have to be a mirror image of the hiring manager to obtain a job offer, but the more connection you make, the greater your likelihood of nailing it.

I have heard of many behind-the-scenes discussions that make or break a person's career. The following are some avoidable derailments:

- **Smelling like smoke.** If the hiring manager is a nonsmoker, don't go into the interview smelling as if you just left the bowling alley on Free Cigarette Night. Many employers avoid hiring smokers due to health insurance.

- **Being overweight.** All things being equal, the more physically fit candidate usually gets hired. I heard a hiring manager say, "She was decent, but needs to lose thirty pounds." Sad but true, I knew this was the deciding factor.

- **Wearing inappropriate attire.** Dress conservatively and in good taste. Men should wear a suit and tie with a starched, long-sleeved dress shirt, with long dark socks and polished shoes. Women should wear a conservative suit or dress without cleavage showing, with the intention of looking professional.

Women and minorities are often at a disadvantage unless the hiring company has a diversity initiative. It is imperative that you know what you're up against. Ask your recruiter if the company is seeking women and/or minorities for the position. It may be an advantage. If not, you have to prepare that much harder. I have personally hired and placed a disproportionate number of women and minorities in jobs. This is due to the fact that women and minorities try harder, are better prepared, and have an attitude of going to get a job versus just getting interviewed.

If you notice differences between you and the hiring manager, don't panic. Try to make as many connections as you can and hope the competition is not too severe.

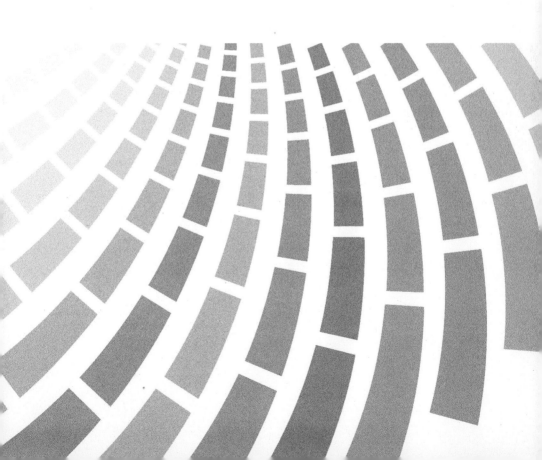

9

Waiting for the Offer

Many books I've read tell you to send a nice thank you note via the mail. If you own any of these books, put them in the recycling bin. The thank you note is best sent via e-mail and done as soon as possible. After the interview, the hiring manager usually makes his or her mind up within twenty-four hours. The antiquated snail mail advice (which could take five to seven days to arrive) becomes irrelevant to a potential offer.

If you interviewed with more than one person, make sure you get a business card from everyone and send each a slightly different note. The more you personalize it with examples from your discussion, the more sincere—and effective—it will be. Your thank you e-mail should only be a few short paragraphs. Here is an actual sample thank you e-mail that was well received—and led to an offer.

Dear Interviewer,

Thank you for taking the time out of your busy schedule yesterday to discuss the opportunity at Company XYZ with

---

me. Company XYZ's marketing provides a competitive advantage for merchants that is underutilized. I believe that Company XYZ's Zap the Consumer product offering is well positioned to capitalize on this opportunity in the marketplace.

My vast experience in both sales management and marketing makes me uniquely qualified for the position. I have worked with several major retailers designing and implementing successful related marketing programs. This experience would enable me to make immediate and valuable contributions to your organization.

I look forward to meeting with you in the near future to further discuss this opportunity.

Again, thank you for your time and consideration.

Sincerely,
Your name

This is a critical step. Proper follow-up is expected; the thank you note is a checklist item for most interviewers. I have seen more than one candidate get clipped because he or she didn't send one. Conversely, I have seen more than one candidate win over a hiring manager who was on the fence by sending a well-written thank you note. It may make the difference in getting you an offer—or not.

OFFER TIME

By this stage, you probably feel as if you have run a marathon. You have placed a great deal of energy on getting to this phase: the offer. It is an exciting time and can be a little nerve-racking. Be grateful you have made it so far and that you are going to receive an offer.

If you do not receive an offer, it is a good idea to send a brief thank you note stating that you "enjoyed all your meetings with such a fine company and please consider me if an opportunity arises in the future." The person receiving the offer may decline it, and an upbeat, professional note may land you the offer next.

Most offers are initially given verbally. Hiring managers either deliver them or have the executive recruiter do it. In either case, and no matter what the offer is, be grateful. Thank him or her for the offer and ask for it to be sent to you in writing (e-mail is preferred) but mention again that you are excited about the prospect of joining such a fine company.

It's time for a little more Psych 101.

TEETER-TOTTER PRINCIPLE

If you have worked with me as a candidate, you have undoubtedly heard of my Teeter-Totter Principle. If you haven't, bear with me. It's a very simple but apropos analogy.

Remember those days on the teeter-totter at the playground? If the other person on the teeter-totter weighed more than you, you were at a significant disadvantage. I hated to be stuck up in the air knowing I would likely crash on my bottom when the other person jumped off. Well, the job search process is like that old teeter-totter.

Before you have an interview, you are up in the air while the hiring manager is firmly on the ground. When you get an interview, you are still up in the air, but at least you're on the teeter-totter. Once you get to the final round of interviews, you are getting closer to the ground but still up in the air. Then, the offer comes. Guess where you are now? You got it: firmly on the ground. And where's the hiring manager? That's right—up in the air.

Keep this in mind: It could have taken several months to get to that offer, and all the while, you were up in the air. Once the offer hits, the hiring manager expects you to say yes on the spot and start the next day. Hiring managers don't like to be up in the air for very long. They never consider the possibility that you may say no to their offer.

Even though you are on the ground, keep this teeter-totter principle in mind. If the offer feels right, answer, "I'm honored to have such a fine offer from you. I'm excited to work for you. Please send me the detailed offer in writing so I can formally say yes as quickly as possible." You gain a psychological advantage by implying acceptance without committing—and buy yourself more time to negotiate the "little things" that matter to you (flex time, paid vacation, etc.).

Put the onus back on the anxious (up in the air) hiring manager, but first tell him or her that you want the job. Delaying your decision will nullify your momentum even if you eventually take the job. A verbal maybe from you is not legally binding anyway—you can always change your mind if the written terms of the offer are not right.

Long live the teeter-totter!

HOW TO AVOID BUYER'S REMORSE AND MAKE THE RIGHT CHOICE

Okay, you've nailed a job offer or maybe even multiple offers. Congratulations. And caution. Huh? Prepare for a roller-coaster ride. I'll explain this with an example we can all relate to: the car buying experience. When you're buying a car—new or used—there's the listed price and the real price. You're not sure how low the seller will go, but you know it's below the listed price. Let's say it's listed at $30,000; you offer $25,000. The seller hems and haws and stomps his feet, but comes back with $28,000; you counter with $26,000, then after another round of haggling, you settle on $27,500. The seller says, "Sold." You feel great that you are getting a nice discount and agree. Driving away in your new car, all of the sudden you say, "I should have offered less." This is buyer's remorse. And its twin appears in most job searches.

It's common to feel panic seep in right before accepting. This is the point when your chatting monkey—that inner voice that is constantly criticizing your every move—takes center stage. The trick is to toss the monkey back in its cage and pay attention to your gut instincts.

Two questions usually emerge at this point:

1.   How do I know this offer is the right one?

2.   Should I take the job even if it doesn't exactly match my dream job description but comes close?

I'll give you the *Reader's Digest* answer that should help you with these two critical questions. Take out a piece of paper and write "Needs" and "Wants" at the top of two columns. Then review your notes from your ideal dream job description from page 15 and fill in this new page with those thoughts as well as anything new that comes to mind. (As before, you may have more or fewer than what we've given you room for here; this is just a starting place for you.) Then rank them in order of importance.

NEEDS	RANK	WANTS	RANK
1. _____	_____	_____	_____
2. _____	_____	_____	_____
3. _____	_____	_____	_____
4. _____	_____	_____	_____
5. _____	_____	_____	_____
6. _____	_____	_____	_____
7. _____	_____	_____	_____

Here's an example:

NEEDS	RANK	WANTS	RANK
Base Salary of at least $75,000	1	Education reimbursement	5
Promotability in 2 years or less	4	Home office	2
Bonus opportunity	3	Stable company	1
Full health benefits	5	3 weeks of vacation	3
Never relocating	2	Stock options	4

If your offer meets all your needs and wants, your decision is a no-brainer. If most of your needs are not met, it's not the right job for you, period. (If you desperately need the money, take the job as a stepping stone but be aware that job hopping can thwart future opportunities.)

But what if all but one or two of your needs are met? If they are low-ranking, take a deep breath and reassess your needs. Could some of these move to the "wants" column? At this point, only you can decide.

Some of life's best decisions are the most difficult ones. What is vital is to follow your gut and back it up with a fact-based assessment like this one. Don't make the mistake of settling for the first thing that comes along if you are having serious doubts, but be aware of the difference between the irrational (i.e., chatting monkey) and rational (your true self).

HOW TO LEAVE YOUR CURRENT COMPANY

What if you're having some doubts about leaving your current company? This is perfectly natural—it's another form of buyer's remorse. What should you do? Never, ever, ever put a gun to your boss's head with, "I have an offer from another company. If you don't match this, I'm outta here." This demand may result in a counteroffer.

What is a counteroffer? It's when you tell your current company that you are resigning and they talk you out of leaving, usually by tossing you more money to stay. If you decide to do an about face and stay, the odds are against you.

The Wall Street Journal had a great article about the pitfalls of counteroffers. They studied 29 people in differing jobs and industries who took counteroffers in a given year. Twenty-seven out of the 29 were either fired, let go, downsized, or right-sized within the first year. The other two were unhappy and were looking furiously for another job. There's a teeter-totteresque explanation for this. Here we go again.

When you tell your boss the two magic words, "I resign," you hope he or she will be the consummate professional and say something like, "We're really going to miss you here, but I am excited for you. Good luck and tell me if there's anything I can do." Nope! Most bosses' first reaction is, "Oh, no, what am I gonna do now? You can't leave me high and dry."

Remember, people usually operate from their id-ego—a selfish state—and automatically take a resignation as a personal affront. They know they will get a hard time from their bosses for losing you. If they've experienced turnover in the past, they also know it will take them six months (on average) to replace you. And, at this point, they will do whatever they can to coax you to stay.

When I resigned from one of the companies I had worked for, they tried to coax me to stay with more money. Ironically, this was the same company that had underpaid me for five of the last seven years, was in a 40 percent downsizing, and had frozen all salary increases. Now, all of a sudden after I found an ideal job with more money and greater responsibility, they could find some dough to throw from those "budgets" that didn't exist earlier.

I said, "Thanks, but no thanks." Had I taken a counteroffer, I know they would have let me go during the downsizing (one of my mentors told me this a couple of years later). I followed my instincts—and they were right.

Counteroffers are nothing more than a short-term fix for your boss to find your replacement! The percentages are stacked against you. If you have taken a counteroffer, turn up your job search before you become another statistical victim.

The worst thing that can happen if you resign with doubts is to have your boss counter with *we were just about to promote you and pay you quite a bit more.* This happens more often than you think. It's a crafty counteroffer, but it's still toxic (re-read the WSJ statistics).

Be 100 percent certain *before* you resign, by saying to your boss, "I'm having career indecision and I wanted to discuss my future, projected responsibilities, including compensation, with you."

Your boss may or may not be truthful to you, but if they were planning on promoting you and paying you more, this is his or her chance to say it—not after you resign. There is no turning back.

Okay, the boss didn't say what you wanted to hear. You can check off that box and have the confidence to move on. So what is the best way to resign? Professionally and with dignity.

Many people do the opposite and later regret it. Saying (or singing), "Take this job and shove it!" may seem like the thing to do, but don't. Regardless of your unhappiness with your soon-to-be ex-boss and company, you have invested too much time and energy there to burn the bridge. Besides, if you get a poor reference years later because you had to let some anger out, was it really worth it?

Proper resignations include the following:

- Resign in person if possible. If not, you should be communicating on the phone "live"—no voicemails or e-mails.

- Have a letter of resignation with you (one paragraph should suffice) with your two weeks' notice spelled out and cc: Human Resources. Keep it professional. No personal attacks.

Dear Mr./Ms. Ex-boss,

I am resigning my position effective (today's date). I will continue to work and help in the transition process in any way I can until my final date of employment: (two weeks from today's date). I am grateful for my experiences at Company ABC and wish you and the company continued success.

Regards,
Happy X. M'Ployee
cc: Hal Phull, Human Resources

The letter of resignation is important. It is a professional way to leave on good terms—your terms. Several bosses, upon hearing you are quitting, will say, "Well, let's just make this your last day. Give me your keys and I'll have you escorted out of the building" (your boss is making it much easier to quit with this selfish response).

By putting in your two weeks' notice, you are legally entitled to two weeks' pay, regardless of whether your boss wants you there or not. They cannot just throw you out the door without your two weeks' pay (plus unused vacation pay)—it's illegal. Resigning properly (in writing) ensures that you will get your two weeks of pay regardless of what your boss may think (this advice is worth at least what you paid for this book and then some).

Let's revisit the boss's response: He or she might lash out at you. People act selfishly and you can use this principle to your advantage. After you (professionally) tell your boss, "I resign," your boss may think, "Oh no, what do I do now?" He or she will likely want to squeeze every bit of juice out of you during your last two weeks—if they even keep you there.

Take the high road: be helpful—within reason—and leverage the situation with what will help you. Your boss needs you now; use this to your advantage. Ask your boss to give you a letter of recommendation on company letterhead. If you get the old I-don't-have-time excuse (complete with a four-letter word), offer to write it yourself on official company stationary and have him or her sign it. One of the best letters of recommendation I ever received was one I had to write on my own.

The letter of recommendation is important for two reasons:

1. It's a great item for your brag book (and to use in future interviews).

2. The moment you leave for the last time, bosses have a tendency of belittling you. Everything that goes wrong for the next six months will be blamed on you, and your name will usually be dragged through the mud. Often, your "resignation" turns into a "we fired him or her." Egos. Having a recent letter of recommendation nullifies negative and harmful gossip.

When resigning, prepare for the worst, but expect the best. Negative thoughts, negative suggestions have no influence over you.

10

Free Career Advice

*

Everybody likes "free stuff"—and free advice is sometimes the best. I can't be a Mystical Career Guide and Life Coach without being able to impart career (and life) advice. I'll give you some sample questions I've been asked and the advice I have given:

Q:
Can I have more than one blissful dream job?

Absolutely! You have seven items on your "narrowed down" *Bliss List* (out of your original 15), so you ideally could have seven dream jobs—or 15 or 20. There are no limits, no boundaries to what you can accomplish if you focus your mind on your goals with enthusiastic confidence and gratitude.

I currently have four blissful dream jobs: writing books, executive search, life coaching, public speaking—and plan on having many more. Keep in mind that it is very difficult to have more than seven things going on in your head at once without frustrating yourself. Once you are in your bliss, you will find that other things that were on your list will magically appear. It may seem to be out of nowhere or a coincidence—at first. Remember, there are no coincidences. The Law of Attraction happens 24/7, whether you believe it (you do) or not.

Q:
Given all your experience, are there any companies you would consider "dream companies" to work for?

I think The Gallup Organization is a terrific company. *How Full Is Your Bucket?* is an easy but powerful book to read—written by Gallup's former Chairman Donald Clifton. Dr. Clifton passed away in 2003, but his legacy of an outstanding culture has continued. Dr. Clifton wrote the book on positive psychology—literally, starting in the 1950s. Then he put it into practice at Gallup. If you want a positive environment (filled with genuine appreciation and gratitude), a low turnover rate, and high employee loyalty and morale, then Gallup is atop the list.

Other fine dream companies to target? This depends on what you're looking for, but a reliable source is available: Fortune's list of the 100 Best Companies to Work For. To pick the 100 Best Companies to Work For, *Fortune* partners with the Great Place to Work Institute to conduct the most extensive employee survey in corporate America; more than 246,000 employees at 280 firms participated in this year's survey, which asks questions related to their attitudes about management's credibility, job satisfaction, camaraderie, pay and benefit programs, and a series of open-ended questions about hiring practices, methods of internal communication, training, recognition programs, and diversity efforts. The top ten from 2012 are these:

1. Google

2. Boston Consulting

3. SAS Institute

4. Wegmans Food Market

5. Edward Jones

6. NetApp

7. Camden Property Trust

8. Recreational Equipment

9. CHG Healthcare Services

10. Quicken Loans

Q:

My daughter is graduating from college soon, can you help her?

Sure! Though I work primarily with senior-level management job searches (usually with total compensation over $100,000), I'd love to help your daughter. What would she like to do?

"She's not sure, but her degree is in business," you say.

Great. The world is her oyster. I'm guessing she has not given much serious thought to what she wants to do with her B.S. (I always think the B.S. is aptly named and funny. For the record, I have a B.A. degree. I didn't get my B.S. until I went into sales.)

My advice is to have her try to find a large company. Which ones? Have her start with the Fortune top 15 companies:

1. Exxon Mobil

2. Wal-Mart Stores

3. Chevron

4. ConocoPhillips

5. General Motors

6. General Electric

7. Berkshire Hathaway*

8. Fannie Mae

9. Ford Motor

10. Hewlett-Packard

11. AT&T

12. Valero Energy

13. Bank of America Corp.

14. McKesson

15. Verizon Communications

* Note: Berkshire Hathaway is a holding company for Warren Buffett's investments. I like several of his perennial favorites like Coca Cola, P & G, Wrigley, and Gillette.

The largest companies offer the greatest opportunities for career growth and are likely to be doing business for the next ten years. Also, they will have extensive college recruitment efforts and salaries that are competitive if not above average.

Your daughter should target these companies with creative networking (I know it may not be easy), direct mail, and via each company's website. Most importantly, find out which of these companies will conduct on-campus interviews and get on the schedule. Many colleges and universities offer a Career Night with sometimes hundreds of companies represented (usually by human resources and/or sales managers), and there just to recruit students. These are a must to attend!

Have your daughter dress in a conservative suit, bring a folder full of résumés, and be first in line. Have her treat these brief meetings as an interview. She should express genuine interest in the company and be brief but effective: "I'm so glad you came here tonight—and that I had a chance to meet you. I am interested in interviewing for a position with your company. What are the next steps?"

This type of interaction opens the door and gives your daughter a card with a phone number and e-mail address for follow-up, plus a face-to-face meeting. Chances are, the person at Career Night will be doing the on-campus interviewing, and your daughter now has left a favorable first impression.

If location doesn't matter, my advice (especially to a college graduate, but applicable to anyone), is move to Bentonville, Arkansas, and get a job with Wal-Mart (there are plenty of positions available in all departments). The training programs that Wal-Mart offers are solid; opportunity for advancement is strong; but salaries for companies looking for people to work with Wal-Mart and live in Bentonville, Arkansas, are way out of whack. You can expect to earn, on average, 30 percent more in salary working for a company (and there are plenty of them) doing business—or wanting to do business—with good ole Wal-Mart. Plus, the cost of living is very low and quality of life is very high.

A couple of years spent in Bentonville will catapult you up corporate ladders with companies. You cannot become a vice president of a consumer goods' manufacturer without Wal-Mart knowledge and experience. They are number one and will stay number one. They already account for more than 20 percent (sometimes 30 to 40 percent) of most of their vendors'/companies' total revenue.

Other locations to consider where salaries are high relative to the cost of living and the quality of life are:

- Redmond, Washington (Microsoft #44)
- Minneapolis, Minnesota (Target #31)
- Cincinnati, Ohio (P&G #23)

Q:
I am a female [or minority] seeking a career change. Can you help me?

Absolutely! Many companies hire recruiters especially for diversity initiatives. Ask your recruiter if he or she is working on any searches for minority candidates. It is usually an advantage to have minority status—which was not the case 30 years ago. Nowadays, however, a qualified minority candidate can sometimes earn a higher salary by lining up multiple offers. The best litmus test is to ask what percentage of employees are minority status in a given company and how many senior managers are minorities. A company with a low percentage of minorities may be a red flag (you'd feel like a unicorn) or a golden opportunity for rapid advancement.

Q:

My ideal job is to be the CEO of a Fortune 500 company. What is the ideal background needed?

Great question. Big company training is paramount to learning the fundamentals and giving you the impressive, blue-chip background. From there, multi-company and multi-industry exposure is critical.

If you can "survive" with one company for your entire career, you are a very rare breed—but not likely a candidate for CEO—with perceived myopic, one-dimensional experience.

The chairman of a Fortune 10 company was asked by an employee, "What would it take for me to become chairman here?"

The chairman retorted, "Leave the company."

He wasn't joking either. Seek multi-company exposure, and when you change companies, commit to yourself that you will do so only if you can ascend to greater responsibility. CEOs become CEOs by making strategic, career-building moves—emulate their actions.

Q:

When is the best time to look for a new job?

While you're gainfully employed. You have the most leverage when you don't have to leave. Companies are looking for successful, well-adjusted, and optimistic people. You are more likely to gain the next step in responsibility and a higher income if you can show an attitude of "I care, but not that much."

If you are unemployed, but are still collecting compensation (severance salary, unused vacation pay, benefits, etc.), consider listing "to Present" on the dates of your last job on your résumé. An interviewer is not likely to ask if you're currently employed if your résumé states "to Present," and you don't have to lie—just don't offer the information.

Q:
What if I'm asked if I'm still employed during the interview and I'm not?

The right answer is to be truthful, but be prepared to give an upbeat explanation as to why. An effective answer is: "As you probably know, my company is in the midst of a sizable layoff. I'm likely to receive an offer for early retirement, even though I'm obviously too young to retire. I am interested in your company and the position regardless of my company's layoff decisions/offers. Ideally, I could time a severance package accordingly."

You were vague enough without directly lying (it's none of their business and has no bearing on the work you would do for them anyway). Plus, there isn't an interviewer around who wouldn't be impressed with your ability to first collect a severance package and then come to his or her company. This answer makes your stock rise in the interviewer's eyes.

If you're queasy about this answer, prepare another one. Avoid any explanation that would knock you out of the running (derogatory comments about your boss, performance issues, etc.). Be concise and upbeat—as if it's a blessing in disguise so you *can devote a full concerted effort to finding a good fit.* Now, if you tried to set your boss on fire but were acquitted, you probably will have a tough time. Write a book (anyone can do that).

Kidding aside, a good strategy is to take the fact that you're unemployed off the table. How? Mention, in vague terms, the *other job offer* you're considering. The risk is minimal. If the hiring manager has already decided to pass, you may hear, "Well, we're not going to be able to decide in time. Take the other offer." If not, the interviewer will sell you on the job he or she is offering (a very good sign!). Now, you're in a position of strength to nail an offer rather than backpedaling.

Q:
How do I know when I am making the right move?

I was asked this question by a friend whose company was just placed on the chopping block (we call it putting up the corporate *For Sale* sign). He was panicky and full of fear for the future (hint, it's not Eckhart Tolle).

He had gotten an offer to work two levels below where he currently was and for a company with a less-than-stellar reputation. He was ready to jump ship and asked for my blessing. My initial reaction was to call him "nuts," but my advice was "make the change only if the job you are accepting would make sense for your career goals, regardless of whether your company is for sale or not."

His fear reflected his insecurity, and he was irrational (not a good reference point). He ended up ignoring my advice and grabbing that job. And he was miserable right away. He only lasted four months—then he was fired.

So, now where is he? Interviewing from the unenviable position of two levels below his actual market value—and unemployed. Applying the Law of Attraction to his case: he got what he wished for.

If a job makes sense whether or not you are unemployed or are about to become unemployed, take the job. Otherwise, set your career goals and keep looking with enthusiastic confidence.

Q:
What makes you a successful executive recruiter?

Two things: I seek quality companies to represent and quality candidates to place.

I only recruit for companies that I would work for myself. Interestingly, I frequently get job offers for the very position from companies looking to use me as their recruiter. I look at companies from all angles.

Sir Warren Buffett is a great inspiration for me. His investment decisions are based on common sense—he needs to really understand and like the products or services of the companies he invests in and they have to have superior management. Finally, he has to be able to predict with certainty where the business will be ten years from now. He is also a voracious reader. He's read more annual reports than anyone. Once he "gets it," he moves quickly. He is rarely wrong.

My target companies (like Buffett's) need to have a competitive advantage (number one or two in their industries), stability, and growth that I believe will happen. I also look for a positive corporate culture with low turnover—the numbers rarely lie. I have worked for (as an employee) and recruited for a large number of privately held companies. They tend to view business in the long term, are very passionate about what they do, have great stability, and have lower-than-average turnover.

Once I'm contracted to work on their behalf as an executive recruiter, I view myself as an employee of the company. I always have enthusiasm for my clients and view them as friends and not clients.

When it comes to candidates, I pride myself on having the highest quality database in the industry. I have built up an impressive list of people by using referrals. When I speak to a candidate I respect, I always ask him or her to recommend other topnotch people, regardless of location and function. "Like attracts like" and good people know other good people who know other good people and on and on.

When I'm given a search assignment, I have the capability to pinpoint A-rated people with a few clicks on my mouse. Using my custom-designed electronic referral notes, I am then targeting people who have been pre-referenced—usually without their knowledge. I always laugh when a hiring company, at offer time, wants to make a reference check as a condition for employment. References provided by the candidate aren't going to reveal any "aha's". Hello—they're provided by the candidate (and if the candidate has a pulse, his or her references are told what to say, making this step useless).

A smart company should require a recruiter to *pre*-reference all potential employees. Earlier, I mentioned the importance of helping a recruiter (only if you trust them) by providing names of good people if you're not interested in the job personally. This is gold for me. You are automatically elevated in my database if you help me. Boomerang?

Quality companies and quality candidates allow me to deliver quality work.

Q:
Will talking to executive recruiters hurt my career?

It shouldn't. A professional executive recruiter would always maintain confidentiality. After reading the earlier section, however, you know that many are not trustworthy. Be careful with information you give out to a recruiter. If he or she doesn't earn your trust, don't trust your personal information with him or her.

As a general rule, do not send your résumé to a recruiter unless he or she identifies the position and company to you and it is something you are interested in pursuing. There are plenty of horror stories about recruiters trying to use a current employee's résumé as leverage to recruit for the very company that pays the paycheck. Be wary of the recruiter who requests your résumé without any specifics.

Q:
Is it safe to send my résumé to an Internet service?

No! Never post your résumé, name, or your identity that may give you away on any Internet service. Human resource departments (and bosses) have been known to scour online services looking for their employees' résumés. Chances are, if a boss spends his time looking for his employees' résumés online rather than working with them, you don't want to work for him anyway. But don't give him a reason to let you go.

Q:
I recently graduated from college and am thinking of getting my master's degree. I have a couple of interesting job offers currently. What should I do?

Isn't it great to have options? There is something to be said for completing all of your education and then obtaining that dream job with advanced degree in hand. In most jobs, the greater the degree, the greater the responsibility—and pay. But given the ridiculous cost of education (especially for a top-tier MBA from a private school), it is a great idea to gain valuable work experience (and a paycheck for a change) and have the company pay for it.

Many companies (especially the larger ones) have fantastic education reimbursement programs. And many graduate programs offer flexible accelerated degrees (with weekend/night combinations).

If you don't mind multi-tasking for 18 months (or fewer in many cases), you can get a free MBA and have a built-in career launch pad once you graduate. Companies will promote you faster when you obtain an advanced degree; they know you are more marketable and could flee to one of their competitors if they don't put you on their fast track.

I took a graduate course toward an MBA degree while working full-time during my first year out of college. I was in the middle of an intensive management training schedule with my company and was actually able to double-dip. I tied in the primary required project for the course (a written case study and presentation to the class) with my management training. I earned an "A" grade and impressed some top brass at the company with my independent research. And it only took a handful of nights during one summer. The company paid for the course, I was promoted a few months later, the course helped, and it was well worth it.

Take the best job offer from the company that has the best education-reimbursement policy and negotiate a graduate degree–reimbursement benefit before you accept the offer (many companies try to make you go through an "approval process" before shelling out money for your courses, especially if it's an expensive executive MBA program).

Q:
Why did you go into business for yourself?

As I transitioned from college/graduate school into the business world, one of my early *Top Seven Bliss List* items was to be self-employed. Every company I worked for was rock solid as I joined, but every single one either sold outright or divested the division I was in. This strengthened my desire to own my own company one day. I figured I may as well start my own company; at least I'll know if it's going to sell.

Q:
I'm 58 years old and looking for a career change. Am I too old?

Don't ever ask a recruiter or potential employer this question. It is illegal for an employer to ask a potential employee his or her age. However, as an executive recruiter, I am asked that question by clients (hiring companies) often, regarding candidates. Legally, I cannot ask age either. It's ironic: it's illegal to ask the question, but you can require the same person to fill out an application for employment and happen to include date of birth. The cold, hard reality of the business world is that youth is desirable.

Generally, hiring managers prefer to hire in their own likeness—looking for similar/same company background/training, hometown, religion, race and/or age group. Remember, like attracts like. In this case, find out the age of the hiring manager (that's not illegal) and his or her boss, and if you think age is an issue, then "modify" your résumé (but don't lie). The hiring manager only needs to look at college degree and date to get an idea of your age. So don't include the year you graduated. Remember, it's your résumé and your marketing document.

The next giveaway is the first year you worked after graduation. Since you have to give at least some years for employment, omit your first ten years after college; chances are, they are irrelevant anyway. You are not lying, just appearing ten years younger—on paper. For the interview, be careful not to divulge dates that would give the nosy interviewer the answer to the "illegal" question. If you are designed to live to 128, being 58 should be the prime of your life, after all.

The irony is that the older employee is generally wiser and, in many cases, more productive and loyal. Napoleon Hill, author of one of the bestselling business books of all time, *Think and Grow Rich,* believed a person made the most intelligent decisions in his or her mid-fifties.

But most companies want young and—implicitly perceived— energetic new hires. The desired formula is to hire someone for five years, work them hard, boot them out the door, and then replace them with a young hot-shot. At all the companies I worked for, there weren't many retirement parties. The days of getting the gold watch at age sixty-five and walking out proudly on your own are over.

Employers are not loyal to employees and vice versa (gives a guy like me in executive search a chance to make a buck or two—or $3 million). This is true in most industries and professions, and is likely to continue or even worsen.

THE QUESTIONS
ABOUT ILLEGAL QUESTIONS

Though it is very useful to learn as much as you can about the hiring manager and his or her boss, never divulge personal information about yourself unless it is to your advantage. It is illegal for an employer to discriminate against you based on your race, gender, religion, marital status, children, family, age, disabilities, ethnic background, country of origin, sexual preferences, or age.

Does it still happen? Sure. But you are not required to answer illegal questions. If asked one, simply say, in a lighthearted way, "I'm not sure we should be discussing this. Can we stick to my skills to do the job you are interviewing me for?"

Any hiring manager who asks these questions is unprofessional, unenlightened, and has poor business etiquette. My advice: turn and run. Do you really want to work there?

Q:
What should I do about unemployment gaps?

First of all, I can't name a single CEO who doesn't have a gap in his or her professional background—it's almost a prerequisite. With all the downsizings and chapter 11's, it is rare to find someone without a gap. That said, it is wise to *disguise* gaps. I didn't say "lie," I said disguise. If asked by the interviewer, you have to answer honestly; but, don't open up the can of worms.

You only have about 45 minutes in an interview, so don't waste the time defending a blip on your background. The issue is how to present yourself. Don't feel like you have to inject sodium pentothal. Remember, your résumé is your marketing brochure. Here's my recommendation:

- Minor gaps—a few months for whatever reason—list your time in years, not months.
- If over a year, consider removing dates entirely and focus on capabilities.
- If terminated, but still receiving compensation, list "to Present" as end date. It is unlawful for a hiring manager to contact your "present" employer without your written consent. If you're still receiving compensation, you are technically still employed and more marketable while still employed.
- If you took time off from the workplace to raise children—like the story of Maria earlier—this raises a red flag. Again, remove dates entirely and focus on capabilities. If asked in an interview, answer concisely—you're probably not the first one to take time off to raise children.
- Chances are, you have some volunteer work you can list during this "gap." Another great gap filler is listing "Management Consultant." It is easy to form a small business: less than $100 in most states.

Your résumé is your invisible first impression, so spend time formatting it to assist you, not hinder you. What if an astute hiring manager uncovers an "aha" gap or gaps, even if not listed on your résumé?

Prepare upbeat answers. If you were terminated for anything short of criminal cause, an HR department will typically only provide the bare minimum on a reference check. They are forewarned, usually in a written policy, to verify dates of employment and job title only. In my career, I was terminated, but it was voluntary. When it came up in an interview, I presented it as a positive—that I was offered a lucrative severance package in lieu of staying on with the acquiring company who had an uncertain future. Never unload on a previous employer or manager; always explain your termination as a massive total department/company-wide change, not a personal vendetta against you.

We've covered a wide gamut of information. I hope you have been formulating and fine-tuning your own career goals. There are plenty of sources for advice—both paid and free. The ultimate barometer for accepting advice is your instinct. If it is right for you, you will feel it. Trust your gut instincts—they are always right.

11

Marching Orders

Dream your job
　　Make it real
First with goals
　　Then with feel
Close your eyes
　　And see the sky
As you fly
　　Don't ask why
The life you choose
　　Unreal may seem
Build your life
　　With your dream

While studying English (and many of the great masters of the language), I told more than one professor that one day I would write and publish a poem. It may not be Shakespeare, but it's mine, and I did it! Touché, Billy-boy.

I have really enjoyed taking you through *The Bliss List*. I hope you are inspired to live the life you were meant to live—with abundance and joy. Combining the mystical (the inner wisdom you have) with the practical (actionable insight) will catapult you into any world you choose to create for yourself.

Buddha said, "An idea that is developed and put into action is more important than an idea that exists only as an idea." Notice ideas that come to you and follow your emotions. If the idea feels good inside, put it into action. You have all the tools to join the one out of five of us who are "happy" in our jobs.

You know that you control it—you have the power to become a disciplined mind, devoid of limitation and toxic thought. You are energetic, abundant, and joyful; the more you unleash your inner core, the better your job—and your life—becomes.

SEE YOUR RETIREMENT PARTY

This exercise is a powerful way to attract your desired dream job. This one involves visualization (best done during meditation or quiet thought).

See yourself seated at the head table for your retirement party. You are electing to retire on your own, and your dream company is honoring you! See each person get up and describe how you touched their lives, accomplished amazing things, and were an inspiration to so many people. Be creative—use your *Bliss List*.

The more realistic you can make your retirement party, the better. Even though you're much older in your visualization, see yourself at your retirement party as vibrant, energetic, and grateful. The more intensely you can feel as if it is really happening, the stronger your vibration, which will ultimately trigger the Universe to answer.

We're nearing the end of the book. One of my initial *Bliss List* items was to help more than 100,000,000 people; thank you for bringing me one step closer to my goal. Life's about the journey, not the destination. Thank you for being part of my journey and for sharing yours with me. Everyone is connected. We are all brothers and sisters; mothers and fathers; or sons and daughters.

I am eternally grateful that you made the time to finish *The Bliss List*. I sincerely hope you are inspired by this book and will try the many things you have read for yourselves. They work. When they work for you—when you obtain your bliss—please tell me your story and what helped you on your journey (I smell a sequel). Send your story to JPHansen@YourBlissList.com, and visit www.BlissList.com for updates.

Mother Teresa said, "God doesn't require us to succeed; He only requires that you try." You have the tools and inspiration; now it's time to try.

Good luck in finding your bliss. Sharing this with you has actually become my newest blissful dream job. Thank you for sharing my dream.

One final note: change is eternal, progress divine. Be your bliss!

Résumé Makeovers

The best way to become a great writer is to first become an avid reader. This holds true in writing résumés. This section will inspire you to design your own killer résumé after reading some real-life examples (names and companies altered).

I'm going to give you a brief background of each person, show you their "before" résumé, then discuss ideas for improvement. Finally, you'll see the finished product, followed by some comments. Ready to get started?

RÉSUMÉ MAKEOVER #1

Meet Barb. Barb was let go (out of the blue and with no warning) from a Fortune 100 pharmaceutical company. She hadn't kept up her résumé (understatement) and was in a bit of a panic when she called me, since she was feeling pressure to obtain employment—and fast.

She was a well-paid sales executive, earning almost $200,000 in the past year. Here is the original résumé she sent me. Does her résumé reflect that she is worth that much? I don't think so.

BARB E. DAHL
31 South Main Street, Anytown, NJ 10012
609-200-0000 cellular • 609-211-1111 home • bdahl@salesqueen.net

EMPLOYMENT:

6/04-8/08	**Pfeel Well Pay More, Inc.,** Anytown, NJ *Senior Therapeutic Specialty Representative* Manage territory consisting of Anytownl/Anytown2: Methodist Hospital, All Well Health System, Anytown: St Elizabeth's Hospital, Bryant East and West, Freeme, Kowtown, and Havenot, New Jersey. Call on specialty physicians, i.e., general surgeons, orthopedic surgeons, neurologists, pain medicine, pulmonary/critical care, hospitalists, and emergency room physicians to increase product use and market share; develop and implement business plan, call cycle, and speaker activities within territory to insure coverage with respect to strategic capabilities; assist DM with training and mentoring two new representatives; support DM with setting up preceptorships and presenting POA topics.
7/02-6/04	**Slimmer Orthopedics,** Anytown, NJ Territory Manager Responsible for selling full line of orthopedic implants and trauma products to 9 hospitals and 2 surgery centers. In charge of negotiating prices for instruments, implants, and competitive conversions. Oversee use of Slimmer Orthopedics re-infusion products with spine and joint surgeons in Anytown. Present in surgery to support surgeons and staff in correct use of Slimmer Orthopedics instruments and implants. Conduct training session for surgical technicians and surgery staff on proper use of Slimmer equipment.
10/96-7/02	**Pfeel Well Pay More, Inc.,** Anytown, NJ Senior Institutional Healthcare Representative Successfully sold all products in a variety of settings including: **Academic Medicine;** University of New Jersey Medical Center, Clarkstein Hospital,Princeton University

Medical Center
Federal Accounts; Anytown VAMC, Skyblue Air Force Base
Long Term Care; Ominouscare, Unicare, Kohlsteins
Managed Care; United Healthcare, Coventry, Blue Cross/Blue Shield

2001 IHR LAT MVPTryit Convention winner 1998
Zittec Convention winner 1998
Arthriticept Convention winner 1997

- 1998 VPC (#1 IHR in Region)
- 1998 Circle of Excellence (#6 in Division)
- 1998 IHR Rookie of the Year
- 1998 IHR Mover and Shaker Award winner
  (greatest change in GAR position)

7/89-10/96   **Wellfunded Financial,** Anytown, NJ
Compliance Auditor (10/95-10/96)
Oversee compliance functions of 28 consumer finance offices in eight Eastern States; perform compliance audits and cash integrity reviews and report findings to District Managers and Executive Officers.

Branch Manager (7 /89-10/95)
Manage and maintain $9 million finance office. Train and supervise staff of 7 in all aspects of daily business; approve and underwrite all lending and insurance decisions; set and oversee goals in order to meet employee and branch objectives; coordinate marketing plans for customers to accomplish branch goals; review all reports concerning trends and dealer activity to access areas of need or concern.

ORGANIZATIONS: International Credit Association
United Way Volunteer
Big Brothers/Big Sisters Volunteer

EDUCATION: **Perfect State College,** Perfect, NJ
Bachelor of Science, May 1989
Major: Business Administration/Marketing
Overall GPA: 3.55/4.0 **Major GPA:**3.76/4.0

- Memorial Basketball Scholarship
- Perfect State College Basketball Scholarship—3 yr letter award
- Perfect State College Baseball Scholarship—3 yr letter award
- Rotary Club-Susie Dingbat Scholarship
- Academic Honors List
- Varsity Club President
- Phi Beta Landing Business Sorority

Did you notice she used sentence descriptions and bullet points for one of her jobs but not the other three? It was the first thing I noticed. And you can bet it would be the first thing the hiring manager would notice—just before she crumples it up and tosses it in the round file. You cannot use an inconsistent format on your résumé, whether you follow my advice or not; it's one or the other.

With this "before" résumé in hand, I spoke with Barb for about a half hour. I quickly realized her résumé didn't reflect how well she was verbalizing her accomplishments. This résumé, by her own admission, was "thrown together quickly." I asked, "Do you want *thrown together quickly* to keep you unemployed *indefinitely*?" Barb didn't laugh. I told her that it wouldn't take her very long to transform her résumé into something she could use with enthusiasm.

Her dilemma (and it wasn't a bad one to have): she had an interview lined up in three days for a great job—a different and more lucrative area of her industry with a well-respected company. She knew she had to work on her résumé—and quickly. I gave her my basic advice: "Use sentences in paragraph form to clearly describe the activities and bullet points to highlight what you accomplished." (Sound familiar? If not, you better turn back to chapter 3 and reread.)

The good news was that the toughest part of the résumé improvement process was over. She mentioned several outstanding accomplishments while we were talking, yet none of them were on her résumé. I told her all she had to do was to add what she had just told me. Later the same day, Barb sent over this improved version:

BARB E. DAHL
31 South Main Street, Anytown, NJ 10012
609-200-0000 cellular • bdahl@salesqueen.net

EMPLOYMENT:

Pfeel Good Pay More, Inc., Anytown, NJ   6/04–Present

Senior Therapeutic Specialty Representative, Anytown, NJ
Manage territory consisting of Anytown1/Anytown2: Methodist Hospital, All Well Health System, Anytown: St Elizabeth's Hospital, Bryant East and West, Freeme, Kowtown, and Havenot, New Jersey. Call on Specialty Physicians: General Surgeons, Orthopedic Surgeons, Neurologists, Pain Medicine, Pulmonary/Critical Care, Hospitalists, Endocrinologists, and Emergency Room Physicians to increase product use and market share; develop and implement business plan, call cycle, and speaker activities within territory to insure coverage with respect to strategic capabilities.

- Ranked #1 (out of 10) in District sales of Zittec—$2.3 million.
- Increased sales by 64% for Zittec over last year in #1 Zip Code, 10010, Anytown, NJ.
- Increased sales by 151% for Zittec over last year in #2 Zip Code, 10011, Beggan Mercy Medical Center.
- Increased Market Share of Zittec by 62.5%.
- Increased Market Share of Vfriend by 12.6% over last year.
- Currently at 110% of Zittec quota (#1 weighted product).
- Successfully launched 9 different dmgs across 4 different medical specialties.

Slimmer Orthopedics, Warsaw, IN   7/02–6/04

Territory Manager, Anytown, NJ
Responsible for selling full line of orthopedic implants and trauma products to 9 hospitals and 2 surgery centers. In charge of negotiating prices for instruments, implants, and competitive conversions. Oversee use of Slimmer re-infusion products with spine and joint surgeons in Anytown. Present in surgery to support surgeons and staff in correct use of Slimmer instruments and implants. Conduct training session for surgical technicians and surgery staff on proper use of Slimmer equipment.

- Ranked #1 in class of 30 for Slimmer hip and knee training in Warsaw, IN.
- Successfully converted Faith Regional Hospital, Norfolk, NE to Slimmer trauma products. Successfully converted #1 Orthopedic Surgeon in Bohmfalk, NJ to Slimmer hip products—took volume from zero to $375,000 in first full year as Territory Manager.
- Increased territory volume from $560,000 to $980,000 in first full year as Territory Manager.

Pfeel Good Pay More, Inc., Anytown, NJ   10/96–7/02

Senior Institutional Healthcare Representative, Anytown , NJ
Successfully sold all products in a variety of settings including: Academic Medicine: University of New Jersey Medical Center, Clarkstein Hospital, Princeton University Medical Center; Federal Accounts: Anytown VAMC, SkyblueAir Force Base; Long Term Care: Ominouscare, Unicare, Kohlsteins; Managed Care: United Healthcare, Coventry, Blue Cross/Blue Shield.

- 2001 IHR LAT MVP.
- Tryit Convention winner 1998.
- Zittec Convention winner 1998.
- Arthriticept Convention winner 1997.
- 1998 VPC (# 1 IHR in Region).
- 1998 Circle of Excellence.
- 1998 IHR Rookie of the Year.
- 1998 IHR Mover and Shaker Award winner (greatest change in GAR position).

Wellfunded Financial, Anytown, NJ   07/89–10/96

Compliance Auditor, 10/95–10/96
Oversee compliance functions of 28 consumer finance offices in eight Eastern States; perform compliance audits and cash integrity reviews and report findings to District Managers and Executive Officers.

Branch Manager   07/89–10/95
Manage and maintain $9 million finance office. Train and supervise staff of seven in all aspects of daily business; approve and underwrite all lending and insurance decisions; set and oversee goals in order to meet employee and branch objectives; coordinate marketing plans for customers to accomplish branch goals; review all reports concerning trends and dealer activity to access areas of need or concern.

ORGANIZATIONS:

United Way Volunteer, 2005–2006
Big Brothers/Big Sisters Volunteer, 2001–2003

ADDITIONAL TRAINING:

Pharmacology One
Pfeel Good Pay More Sales
Pfeel Good Pay More Institutional Selling IV
Pfeel Good Pay More Specialty Selling V
Targeted Selection
Associate Sales Director I
Evelyn Wood Speed Reading
"Converting to Yes" Pfeel Good Pay More Advanced Sales

EDUCATION:

Perfect State College, Perfect, NJ Bachelor of Science, May 1989
Major: Business Administration/Marketing
Overall GPA: 3.55/4.0 **Major GPA:** 3.76/4.0

- Memorial Basketball Scholarship
- Perfect State College Basketball Scholarship—3 yr letter award
- Perfect State College Baseball Scholarship—3 yr letter award
- Rotary Club-Susie Dingbat Scholarship
- Academic Honors List
- Varsity Club President
- Phi Beta Landing Business Sorority

PERSONAL: Married, 1 child

Notice a difference? Barb had articulated all of her accomplishments well, and now she listed them on her most important step in the process—the résumé. She created more space and gave the résumé a full appearance by putting the titles below the respective companies and moving the dates of employment. She made the date of her last job "Present," which got her over that hurdle of explaining why she wasn't with the company anymore (she was still collecting a paycheck in the form of severance pay and unused vacation pay so, technically, she was still there).

She blocked the right side of her résumé to match the left by changing from "left justify" to "full justify" (from the Microsoft Word toolbar). She added "Additional Training" which shows the interviewer that Barb is well-trained.

I wasn't a fan of Barb's original "Organizations" section. It's never advantageous to tell a future employer that you are loaded up with outside, time-consuming, and unrelated interests. Barb wanted to show her philanthropic side, so we compromised by scaling it back to two organizations, and we put it in the past tense by placing end dates on each one. This tells the employer, "Hey, I'm a good person and volunteered for two very important causes, but I'm free and clear now to put all my energies toward working for you."

These résumé changes were not too severe, but it was the difference between getting a blissful dream job paying over $200,000 versus not even getting an interview. It took Barb less than one hour to make these changes. The result: she nailed it and won the job offer! I would say this was a good return on investment.

RÉSUMÉ MAKEOVER #2

Meet Pat Peoples. In sales jargon, Pat was what we call a hunter—a good thing (as opposed to farmer, or not desirable). Pat had several impressive cold-call success stories, after a dot com turned into a dot bomb—like many others at the time. Pat's earnings had been in the low six figure range for the past few years until "Perfectmix" decided to clip the commission structure. Pat was in a panic and wanted my help to find a dream job.

The following is Pat's original résumé:

BEFORE

Pat Peoples
1700 N. Capital Blvd. • Anyplace, TX 78746 • (310) 706-0123 • patpeoples@always.com

OBJECTIVE

A challenging career in outside sales where I can utilize my extensive experience and skills in sales, marketing, communication, and networking to achieve the highest company, career, and personal goals.

SUMMARY

- Over ten years of successful sales experience with six years in solution selling (multimedia, print, e-commerce advertising, and search engine optimization and marketing services)
- Proven ability to increase sales and maximize profitability by:
  - » Creating and implementing innovative sales strategies and customized product/service offerings and proposals
  - » Consistently building a solid pipeline of qualified prospects by cold calling, cultivating leads and developing referrals
  - » Establishing strong, long-term client and agency relationships through excellent customer service
  - » Maintaining extensive product and market knowledge
- Adept at cold calling, prospecting, negotiating & closing business, and account management/development
- Ability to manage existing operations through changes in technology, product repositioning, and various financial environments
- Effective leader, self-starter, problem-solver, and team player dedicated to exceeding goals
- Proficient in Microsoft Office (Word, Excel, PowerPoint, Outlook) sales management software, and numerous software, hardware, and Internet products /services

- Knowledge of online advertising technologies, including third party ad serving, rich media, and emerging ad-targeting and search technology

PROFESSIONAL EXPERIENCE

Perfectmix, Chicago, IL   **2006 to present**
(Performance-Based Marketing Division of Demonink)
Account Executive South West Region
- Develop and close deals with top brand marketers to sell their products/services via Perfectmix Paid
- Search Marketing, Search Engine Optimization, and Affiliate Marketing Services
- Work collaboratively and effectively with all levels of staff including senior management, marketing, and external strategic business partner contacts at Google and Yahoo! & top advertising agencies
- Construct customized presentations and proposals using competitive intelligence and marketing data from third party resources such as BitWise, AdGooRoo, Forrester, Yahoo! Buzz, & Comscore
- Present proprietary search technology and competitive advantages to Vice Presidents of Marketing of top retailers and companies such as CBS, Epson, Disney, Mazda, Countrywide, Guess, Toyota, etc.
- Accomplishments:
  » Achieved quarterly business objectives and sales goals

Los Angeles Grind, Los Angeles, CA   **1999 to 2006**
Senior Account Executive
- Aggressively developed Southern California market for Internet recruiting services, banner advertisements, and multi media campaigns for Fortune 500 and 1000 companies
- Launched Careerbuilder.com in So. California market in 1999; successfully grew Los Angeles Grind market share to become the #1 Tribune newspaper for Careerbuilder sales for five consecutive years
- Educated VP's, decision makers and agencies to emerging online technology and innovation while supporting the benefits and need for multimedia recruitment and branding strategies
- Repositioned competitive role against industry leaders such as Monster.com and HotJobs.com
- Trained, mentored, and motivated Recruitment Classifieds Division to drive sales by developing sales skills and online advertising product knowledge
- Most sales involve annual or semi-annual commitment. Client list includes Boeing, Mitsubishi, Healthnet, Northrop Grumman, Corinthian Colleges, Ameriquest
- Accomplishments and Awards:
  » Achieved #1 Online Sales Person Classifieds Division 2004; 132% Quota 2005
  » Exceeded yearly quota for 5 consecutive years by 128% to 165%
  » Awarded Los Angeles Times 2001 Online Sales Person of the Year
  » Earned #1 Sales Person CalendarLive 1999, 2000

GoodFood.com, San Francisco, CA   **1997 to 1999**
Regional Sales Representative
- Established new Southern California territory and collaborated in designing the
    sales strategy and training collateral that grew company sales force from 4 to
    60 representatives nationwide
- Executed sales through effective cold calling, canvassing, lead generation, and
    referral programs
- Created and implemented regional sales and marketing strategies to consistently
    grow new customer base to 180 new customers first year
- Clients consisted of numerous restaurant chains including Dominos, Brinker
    International, Patina
- Accomplishments and Awards:
    » Produced top sales in the region and 4th in the nation (out of 60 sales
        representatives) in 1998 generating 9.2% of the company's annual revenue

Equiscam International, Inc., Las Vegas, NV   **1995 to 1997**
Sales and Marketing Representative
- Conducted sales presentations, product trainings, and negotiated contracts with
    clients
- Serviced existing accounts which included restaurants, real estate developers, and
    other commercial businesses
- Established and expanded client database through cold calling and client referral
    programs
- Accomplishments:
    » Achieved the ranking of the top 3 sales representative in the nation June 1996

EDUCATION

BS Psychology / Cum Laude Texas A&M University 1993
2001-2005 Careerbuilder.com Bi-annual Training Seminars
2000 Non-Manipulative Selling
1999 SPIN Selling
1993-1994 University of North Texas
        Masters Graduate Program

This résumé would not get to the top of the pile, and it may find the round file. Like Barb's original, Pat's was lacking accomplishments. It was overkill on bullet points, but they were not used to accentuate accomplishments. Using bullet points for everything dilutes their impact.

I'm also not a big fan of the "Objective" as I discussed earlier. They're usually too general (like Pat's) and don't really add anything. If an item on a résumé doesn't add anything, it detracts from your first impression. The proper "Objective" would be listing your ideal job by title, but it is not a needed item. My advice is to get rid of it and use the extra space for impactful accomplishments.

I also don't like the "Summary." It says, "I know you won't really read my résumé so I'll give you the same information twice." Lose the "Summary" and stick with the recommended format: list activities in sentence form, and then bullet-point your accomplishments in order of importance.

In addition, Pat's résumé was convoluted, bouncing around with accomplishments and responsibilities with no cohesiveness. It also employed passive words like *executed, implemented, conducted,* and *serviced.* If you are trying to paint yourself as a hard-charger and a winner, then passive words won't cut it. Not many employers say, "Get me someone who is a good implementer! A real executer. Someone who can conduct things and service an existing client."

I knew Pat well enough to know Pat was a hunter, not a farmer. After speaking with Pat for a half hour, the résumé didn't jive. I suggested that Pat use action words such as *successfully sold, created, developed, obtained, ranked #1, earned,* and *launched.*

Check out the makeover:

AFTER

Pat Peoples
1700 N. Capital Blvd. • Anyplace, TX 78746 • (310) 706-0123 • patpeoples@always.com

PROFESSIONAL EXPERIENCE

Perfectmix, Chicago, IL   2006 to present
(Performance-Based Marketing Division of Demonink)

Account Executive - Southwest Region

Responsible for Sales of Perfectmix Paid Search Marketing, Search Engine Optimization, and Affiliate Marketing Services targeting U.S. Companies. Primarily target C-Level executives at Fortune 500 Companies using competitive intelligence and marketing data from 3rd party resources such as BitWise, AdGooRoo, Forrester, Yahoo!, Buzz, & Comscore.

- Increased revenue by 217%.
- Ranked #1 out of 14 Account Executives.
- Obtained new business with ABC Corporation, accounting for $1.2 million in new revenue.
- ABC Corporation became Perfectmix's most profitable customer in year one.
- Obtained new business with 123 Incorporated worth an incremental $1.1 million.
- Won Circle of Excellence Trip Award.

Los Angeles Grind, Los Angeles, CA   1999 to 2006

Senior Account Executive

Responsible for the Southern California market for Internet recruiting services, banner advertisements, and multimedia campaigns for Fortune 500 and 1000 companies. Client target list includes Boeing, Mitsubishi, Healthnet, Northrop Grumman, Corinthian Colleges, and Ameriquest. Launched Careerbuilder.com in So. California market in 1999.

- Achieved #1 Online Sales Person out of 13 in the Classifieds Division 2004.
- Exceeded yearly quota for 5 consecutive years by 128% to 165%.
- Obtained a 132% increase versus Quota in 2005.
- Awarded Los Angeles Grind's 2001 Online Sales Person of the Year.
- Successfully increased Los Angeles Grind market share to become the #1 Tribune newspaper for Careerbuilder sales for five consecutive years.
- Ranked #1 Sales Person for CalendarLive in 1999, 2000.

GoodFood.com, San Francisco, CA   1997 to 1999

Regional Sales Representative

Responsible for United States Business Development targeting the restaurant industry in a start-up environment. Designed the sales strategy and training collateral for new markets.

- Obtained 180 new customers in year one, including Dominos, Brinker International, and Patina, which led to an incremental $2 million in revenue.
- Produced #1 sales in the Region and ranked #4 out of 60 nationally in 1998.
- Built company sales force from 4 to 60 Regional Sales Representatives through a 7-member multi-functional team effort.

Equiscam International, Inc., Las Vegas, NV   1995 to 1997

Sales and Marketing Representative

Primary responsibilities include managing the existing client base and developing new business in the Restaurant, Real Estate Developer, and other Commercial Businesses.

- Ranked #3 out of 57 Sales and Marketing Representatives in the nation in 1996.
- Obtained over $1.1 million in new business with Sysco Distributors, servicing T.G.I. Fridays and Benningtons.

ADDITIONAL TRAINING

Careerbuilder.com Bi-annual Training Seminars, 2001–2005
Non-Manipulative Selling, 2000
SPIN Selling, 1999

EDUCATION

University of North Texas
Masters Graduate Program (completed 30 credit hours)
GPA: 3.4/4.0

Texas A&M University
BS Psychology
Cum Laude Honors; GPA: 3.3/4.0

Did you see how we cleaned up Pat's résumé, making the accomplishments hard-hitting and meaningful? We consistently used strong action words to describe accomplishments. This résumé became much clearer and more concise. Pat was thrilled with the improvements, which took less than a half-hour. The result: job offer and dream job!

RÉSUMÉ MAKEOVER #3

Meet Ken Dahl. Ken was bright and driven, but had gaps in his résumé that he felt were hurting his chances of finding gainful employment, let alone his dream job. I agreed. Ken had been let go twice during his career: once due to a corporate downsizing; the other due to cause—he fought the law and the law won (i.e., took on his boss and lost). Here's the original résumé:

KEN DAHL
21 East 51ˢᵗ Street, #1234, New York, NY 10000 • (212) 867-5309 • KenDahl@mattelmale.com

EDUCATION

University of Nowhere, New York, NY   1976 - 1981
Business Administration Bachelor of Science degree

BUSINESS EXPERIENCE

HIDDEN CARBS FOODS, New York, NY   **Feb. 2006–March 2012**
Senior vice-president sales, New York, NY
Solely responsible for sales, sales operations, customer service, analysis, marketing, production, trade shows, forecasting, accounts payables, etc.
- Single handedly grew dollar revenues from $0 to $2.0M in 3 years without any marketing dollars.
- Sold Wal-flower, Costmore, Food Tiger, Stop, Shop & Listen, Wakefull, Safepath, Paymore, and Hole Foods
- Developed "in-store demonstration" training programs tailored for each retail account and hired personnel to execute. Exceeded retailer's sales volume objectives on a per store basis by 250%.
- Hired and managed 15 distributor organizations.

COMMUNION WAFERS CO., New York, NY   **May 1993–July 1998**
Vice-president sales, New York, NY
Managed over $250 million of sales for the company in the United Sates. Recruited, trained, and developed 14 managers including six regional, eight direct/broker sales, one category management, one shelf technology and 20 broker organizations.
- Awarded "Employee of the Year" in 1996.
- Increased net profit by 30%+ for the past three consecutive years, thereby achieving record highs for the company.
- Restructured sales force to improve business with key, strategic customers.
- Led design team to restructure key departments that support sales.
- Helped develop account pro-forma reports.
- Developed sales training manual and factbook. Led sales efforts to establish company's policies and procedures.
- Awarded Wafer Supplier of the Year from Krocker, Al Bertson's, Paymore, OffTarget, and Wal-flower.
- Promoted 5 managers to regional vice-presidents and two customer service managers to account managers.

PROMOTE & GAMBLE, Sincinnati, OH   **Aug. 1981–April 1993**
Director of Sales
Developed and successfully managed three major national new item introductions, including development of all classes of trade marketing strategies. This included sales meetings, sales aids, presentations, and budgets. Promoted three managers.
- Responsible for all aspects involving Test Market/National Introduction. Results were one of largest/fastest market share gains in company's history.
- Sold new channel account and wrote largest single new order in history of company.
- Initiated/ led task force to start first diversity training program in company.

Division Manager, New York, NY
Managed sales of $75 million in the New York Metro area. Recruited and trained 22 sales people and managed one personal account. Promoted 6 people.
- Youngest Division Manager in company's history.
- Set district record by exceeding quota three consecutive years while reducing personnel by 33%.
- Established multi-functional customer service team improving service levels from 65% to 90%.
- Responsible for recruiting at Boston College, Harvard, Dartmouth, Brown, Wellesley, Princeton, and Cornell. One of five featured in corporate recruiting video.

Manager, Sales Merchandising and Sales Training School, Cincinnati, OH
First manager to hold two job functions. Developed sales merchandising programs and materials for new item introductions, consumer promotions/overlays for multiple brand group events, analyzed specific sales results and coordinated training schools for new sales representatives and unit managers. Projects included national new item introductions and the first computerized shelf program, and a national award-winning consumer in-pack promotion.

Unit Manager, New Orleans, LA

Sales Representative & District Field Representative, New Orleans, LA

Ken's résumé has a couple of glaring problems. One, he's revealing his age right away by giving us the year he graduated (and that it took him five years to obtain his degree). This was problematic since most of the hiring managers he targeted were younger. The biggest problem is the two major gaps in his employment history. First, that he's been unemployed since March 2012. The second gap spans nearly eight years, from July 1998 to February 2006.

In talking with Ken, his explanation of the eight year gap was a bit shaky. He was let go from Communion Wafers Company for cause (I'll call it a "personality conflict" with his boss since I can't use his actual verbiage in this book). He actually started his own consulting business which did well for a few years, then took a downturn due mainly to an economic slump. This guy was a high flyer at one point, rapidly ascending corporate ladders with ease. Then, like many others, his career stalled and hit a few snags—but none that should eliminate his consideration for employment.

Here's Ken's new résumé:

KEN DAIIL

21 East 51ˢᵗ Street, #1234, New York, NY 10000 • (212) 867-5309 • KenDahl@mattelmale.com

BUSINESS EXPERIENCE

HIDDEN CARBS FOODS, New York, NY   Feb. 2006–Present

Senior Vice President Sales, New York, NY

- Responsible for sales, sales operations, customer service, analysis, marketing, production, trade shows, forecasting, and accounts payables.
- Increased factory sales from $0 to $2.0M in 3 years with limited marketing support.
- Sold Wal-flower, Costmore, Food Tiger, Stop, Shop & Listen, Wakefull, Safepath, Paymore, and Hole Foods.
- Developed "in-store demonstration" training programs tailored for each retail account and hired personnel to execute. Exceeded retailer's sales volume objectives on a per store basis by 250%.
- Hired and managed 15 distributor organizations.

KEN DAHL CONSULTING, INC, New York, NY   1998–2006

President and Founder

Consulted for several entrepreneurial start-ups on go-to-market strategy, corporate structure, SKU assessment, customer prioritization, category insight management, marketing plans, and finance. Developed account penetration action plans.

- Developed Company XYZ from start-up to profitable within its first two years.
- Designed corporate structure incorporating an indirect sales force for Anywho, Inc. which saved over $7 million in operating expenses.
- Designed marketing plans for WhoKnew Corporation which led to market leadership positions in four categories.
- Secured top-to-top meetings with key customers for 14 client companies, resulting in over $50 million in new revenue.

COMMUNION WAFERS COMPANY, New York, NY   1993–1998

Vice President Sales, New York, NY

- Managed over $250 million of sales for the company in the United Sates. Recruited, trained, and developed 14 Managers, including six regional, eight direct/broker sales, one category management, one shelf technology and 20 broker organizations.
- Awarded "Employee of the Year" in 1996.
- Increased net profit by 32.4% for the past three consecutive years, record highs for the company.

- Restructured sales force to improve business with key, strategic customers.
- Led design team to restructure key departments that support sales.
- Helped develop account pro-forma reports.
- Developed sales training manual and factbook. Led sales efforts to establish company's policies and procedures.
- Awarded Wafer Supplier of the Year from Krocker, Al Bertson's, Paymore, OffTarget, and Wal-flower.
- Promoted 5 Managers to Regional Vice Presidents and two Customer Service Managers to Account Managers.

PROMOTE & GAMBLE, Sincinnati, OH   1981–1993

Director of Sales, Sincinnati, OH

Developed and successfully managed three major national new item introductions, including development of all classes of trade marketing strategies. This included sales meetings, sales aids, presentations, and budgets. Promoted three managers.

- Responsible for all aspects involving Test Market/National Introduction. Results were one of largest/fastest market share gains in company's history.
- Sold new channel account and wrote largest single new order in history of company.
- Initiated/led task force to start first diversity training program in company.

Division Manager, New York, NY

Managed sales of $75 million in the New York Metro area. Recruited and trained 22 sales people and managed one personal account. Promoted 6 people.

- Youngest Division Manager in company's history.
- Set district record by exceeding quota three consecutive years while reducing personnel by 33%.
- Established multi-functional customer service team improving service levels from 65% to 90%.
- Responsible for recruiting at Boston College, Harvard, Dartmouth, Brown, Wellesley, Princeton, and Cornell. One of five featured in corporate recruiting video.

Manager, Sales Merchandising and Sales Training School, Cincinnati, OH

First manager to hold two job functions. Developed sales merchandising programs and materials for new item introductions, consumer promotions/overlays for multiple brand group events, analyzed specific sales results and coordinated training schools for new sales representatives and unit managers. Projects included national new item introductions and the first computerized shelf program, and a national award-winning consumer in-pack promotion.

Unit Manager, New Orleans, LA

Sales Representative & District Field Representative, New Orleans, LA

EDUCATION

University of Nowhere, New York, NY
Business Administration Bachelor of Science degree
G.P.A. in major: 3.2/4.0

PROFESSIONAL DEVELOPMENT

Completed the following seminars:

- Levinson's Institute on Executive Leadership Skills
- Buying Skills Seminar by Dr. Brian Harris
- Presentation Skills by Communispond
- Managing Cultural Diversity by Banks
- Category Management by The Partnering Group
- Strategic Planning by The Boston Group

Reminding Ken that his severance package lasted several months, I had him change the end date for his most recent job to "Present," to avoid the first red flag. Next, I encouraged Ken to include his lost eight years on his résumé. His consulting business was impressive, especially for the first five years. He used general accomplishments rather than getting caught up in annual ones—which would have shown a negative trend. Moving his education to the end, above the new "Professional Development" section, made a difference. His overall G.P.A. was below 3.0, but as you can see, in his major, he was above the cut line. Adding the Dean's List distinction enhanced the "Education" section, and eliminating his five year stay was a no-brainer.

In addition, he did a few minor clean-ups. On his "before" résumé, Ken had treated his titles inconsistently, using different type treatments and capitalizing some but not all of them (*"Vice-president sales"* versus *"**Director of Sales**"*). I favor capitalizing all titles for emphasis, but whatever you do, make it consistent! Overall, the résumé makeover didn't take Ken much more than a half-hour, but proved to be the difference between nailing two job offers versus prolonged and agonizing unemployment.

RÉSUMÉ MAKEOVER #4

Meet Donna Gainer. Donna was a life coach client of mine who was interested in changing industries—after a thirteen-year employment gap. Donna was a teacher who took time off to raise two kids full-time while nearly obtaining her Master's Degree in her spare time. Her Bliss List led her toward a career in professional counseling. Most people would talk themselves out of the possibility before even trying. Donna was no exception. She polluted her mind with self-imposed limitations ("it's a poor economy, who would hire a woman in her late forties after being unemployed for so long?, I have no training in counseling," etc.) Blah, blah, blah. In Donna's favor, she had almost completed her Master's Degree in Professional Counseling, was personable, and had experience working with children in the age group she was targeting as a counselor. But, in spite of all this, she nearly gave up without trying. By now, you know my patience level for fear, lame excuses, and limitations.

Once I convinced Donna that she could do it, and she believed it, it didn't take her long. She completed the two additional courses that gave her the educational credentials required. Now all she needed was to present herself with a résumé.

Here's her original résumé, used for teaching jobs:

BEFORE

DONNA GAINER
123 Cherry Grove St., Columbia, SC • (803) 867-5309 • donnagainer@gmail.com

OBJECTIVE

To obtain a substitute teaching position in elementary, middle, and high school where I can utilize my teaching and counseling experience to help meet the social, emotional and educational needs of students. I am committed to providing an environment that will facilitate enthusiastic learning for all students.

EXPERIENCE

Reading Intervention Teacher   *1990-2001*
Cincinnati Schools, OH

- Develop assessment driven lessons based on Ohio Content Standards, work collaboratively with colleagues, and promote home literacy.
- Design lessons rich in language and literacy learning opportunities, high in student engagement, and multi-sensory.
- Work collaboratively with colleagues and supervisors collecting data and revising teaching strategies to meet district standards and student high interest.
- Responsible for teaching early literacy to first and second graders.
- Instrumental in creating and establishing the reading intervention program for Cincinnati Schools since the inauguration.

Reading Teacher   *1997-1998*
Cincinnati Schools, OH
Assessment driven, individualized and small group instruction.

Kindergarten Teacher   *1993-1995*
Cincinnati Schools, OH
Research-based literacy instruction including guided reading, guided writing, Phonemic awareness, interactive writing, Readers Theater and oral language expression.

Fourth Grade Teacher   *1991-1999*
Cincinnati Schools, OH
- Assumed responsibility for self contained and departmentalized instruction.
- Developed inquiry approached science based lessons to support curriculum standards.
- Served on an interviewing team for hiring staff.

First Grade Teacher   *1987-1991*
Cincinnati Schools, OH
- Literacy based guided reading determined by individual reading levels.
- Opened a new elementary building: responsible for ordering materials, establishing programs, and working collaboratively to assure student needs were being met.
- Supervised Classroom Student Teachers.

First Grade Teacher   *1986-1987*
Cincinnati Schools, OH

Substitute Teacher   *1985-1986*
Served as long term substitute teacher.

EDUCATION

University of South Carolina, Columbia, SC   *2004-Present*
Master of Arts in Professional Counseling

University of Cincinnati, Cincinnati, OH   *May 1999*
Master's Degree in School Counseling
GPA 4.00

Miami of Ohio University, Oxford, OH   *May 1984*
Bachelor of Science Degree in Education, High Honors
Major: Elementary Education, Grades 1–8

The challenge was less daunting than she imagined. To me, the biggest point to emphasize was her Master's degree in Professional Counseling and to de-emphasize the dates. This is what we came up with:

DONNA GAINER

123 Cherry Grove St., Columbia, SC • (803) 867-5309 • donnagainer@gmail.com

EDUCATION

University of South Carolina, Columbia, SC
Master of Arts in Professional Counseling
GPA: 4.0/4.0

University of Cincinnati, Cincinnati, OH
Master's Degree in School Counseling
GPA: 4.0/4.0

Miami of Ohio University, Oxford, OH
Bachelor of Science Degree in Education, High Honors
Major: Elementary Education, Grades (1-8)

RELEVANT TEACHING EXPERIENCE

Reading Intervention Teacher, Cincinnati Schools, OH
- Develop assessment driven lessons based on Ohio Content Standards, work collaboratively with colleagues, and promote home literacy.
- Design lessons rich in language and literacy learning opportunities, high in student engagement, and multi-sensory.
- Work collaboratively with colleagues and supervisors collecting data and revising teaching strategies to meet district standards and student high interest.
- Responsible for teaching early literacy to first and second graders.
- Instrumental in creating and establishing the reading intervention program for Cincinnati Schools since the inauguration.

Reading Teacher, Cincinnati Schools, OH
Assessment driven, individualized and small group instruction.

Kindergarten Teacher, Cincinnati Schools, OH
Research-based literacy instruction including guided reading, guided writing, Phonemic awareness, interactive writing, Readers Theater and oral language expression.

Fourth Grade Teacher, Cincinnati Schools, OH
- Assumed responsibility for self contained and departmentalized instruction.
- Developed inquiry approached science based lessons to support curriculum standards.
- Served on an interviewing team for hiring staff.

First Grade Teacher, Cincinnati Schools, OH

Substitute Teacher
Served as long term substitute teacher.

Donna's résumé no longer screamed "out of work"—we dropped all the dates. In any case, being out of work didn't matter as much as she feared. She was able to secure three interviews and ended up nailing two offers. Changing industries also wasn't as difficult as she thought. The employers were impressed with her teaching experience and even more impressed with how well she presented herself. Having the educational credentials were the only true prerequisite.

Have you seen enough sample résumés yet? I hope the before and after examples were compelling and made you want to take another look at your résumé. I'm constantly asked to write or review résumés for people. Even with bestselling résumé advice, people still fear (four-letter word!) creating their own résumé. Follow this template and in no time, you'll have a first draft of your own killer résumé. All you have to do is fill in the blanks:

Name: _____

Street Address: _____

City, State, Zip Code: _____

Cell phone number: _____

Professional Experience

Most recent employer: _____

Month, Year of start – Present: _____

Current Job Title: _____

Month, Year – Present: _____

Describe what you do in three sentences (responsibility, scope, industry, points of relevance) _____

_____

_____

List greatest accomplishment (remember to quantify and qualify it)

_____

_____

List second greatest accomplishment _____

_____

_____

List third greatest accomplishment _____

_____

_____

List fourth greatest accomplishment _____

_____

_____

List fifth greatest accomplishment _____

_____

_____

Next company (if different) or *next job title:* _____

Month, Year of start – Present: _____

Job Title (if different company): _____

Month, Year – Present: _____

Describe what you do in three sentences (responsibility, scope, industry, points of relevance) _____

_____

_____

List greatest accomplishment (remember to quantify and qualify it)

_____

_____

List second greatest accomplishment _____

_____

_____

List third greatest accomplishment _____

_____

_____

And so on for the companies you have worked for and various positions you have held.

Additional Training

List most impressive applicable training you have received by title and date_____

_____

List second most impressive applicable training you have received by title and date _____

_____

List third most impressive applicable training you have received by title and date _____

_____

List fourth most impressive applicable training you have received by title and date _____

_____

List fifth most impressive applicable training you have received by title and date _____

_____

Education

College or University Name _____

Year started – year finished if 4 years; if not, list year finished _____

_____

Degree(s) _____

_____

GPA (if over a 3.0 out of 4.0 scale, list it; if not, they assume you have the John Belushi GPA) _____

Honors (Magna, Summa, or Cum Laude if it applies to you) _____

_____

_____

Financed percentage of education costs through part-time work—list if over 50%. _____

_____

Personal

Married, number of children is desirable; if thrice divorced and living in a van down by the river, skip it!

* * *

Congratulations—you've just written your résumé. Now, sleep on it, let your subconscious take over (dream programming time!), and see how it improves over the next few days. You'll probably be able to tighten up your descriptions and may come up with some new accomplishments or at least quantify and qualify them better. Compare this first draft with your finished product—your final should be a killer résumé.

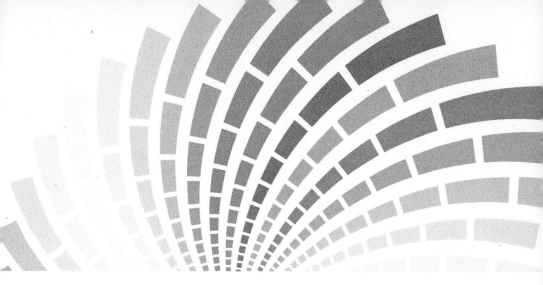

Read More

I am forever grateful and connected to the following pieces of wisdom I have been lucky enough to read, listen to, and watch. Although this is not the complete list, the following have had a profound effect and influence on me.

MYSTICAL BOOKS

Abraham DVD Series by Esther and Jerry Hicks

Ask and It Is Given by Esther and Jerry Hicks

The Bible

Buddha—A Story of Enlightenment by Deepak Chopra

Burt Goldman Mindbox CD Series by Burt Goldman

Chicken Soup for the Soul by Jack Canfield and Mark Victor Hansen

Conversations with God by Neale Donald Walsch

Don't Sweat the Small Stuff by Richard Carlson, PhD

Energy Medicine by Donna Eden

The Eye of the I by David Hawkins, MD, PhD

The Genie Within by Harry Carpenter

The Heart of the Buddha's Teaching by Thich Nhat Hanh

The Hidden Messages in Water by Dr. Masaru Emoto

How Full Is Your Bucket? by Tom Rath and Donald O. Clifton, PhD

Inner Skiing by Timothy Gallwey

Inner Tennis by Timothy Gallwey

Jose Silva Mind Control CDs—9 CD set by Jose Silva

Jose Silva's Everyday ESP by Jose Silva, Jr.

The Law of Attraction by Esther and Jerry Hicks

The Law of Attraction in Action DVD by Esther and Jerry Hicks

Mark Twain's Helpful Hints for Good Living by Mark Twain

Mars and Venus Diet and Exercise Solution by John Gray

Mission by Mark Link, SJ

A New Earth by Eckhart Tolle

Order Out of Chaos by Ilya Prigogine

The Passion Test by Janet Bray Attwood and Chris Attwood

The Pendulum Kit by Sig Lonegren

The Power of Now by Eckhart Tolle

Power vs. Force by David Hawkins, MD, PhD

Psycho Cybernetics by Dr. Maxwell Maltz

Quantum Reality: Beyond the New Physics by Nick Herbert

The Quantum World: Quantum Physics for Everyone by Kenneth Ford

Seasons of the Spirit by Sally Coleman and Maria Porter

The Secret DVD and book (both the same content) by Rhonda Byrne

The Sedona Method by Hale Dwoskin

Self Mastery Through Conscious Autosuggestion by Emile Coue

Seth Speaks by Jane Roberts

The Power of Myth by Joseph Campbell

The Shift DVD by Dr. Wayne Dyer

The Silva Mind Control Method by Jose Silva

Think and Grow Rich (original 1937 version) by Napoleon Hill

Three Magic Words by U.S. Andersen

Way of the Peaceful Warrior by Dan Millman

What The Bleep Do We Know? DVD

You the Healer by Jose Silva and Robert B. Stone

Your Body Doesn't Lie by Dr. John Diamond

BUSINESS BOOKS

The 100 Best Companies to Work For in America by Robert Levering and Milton Moskowitz

The Art of War by Sun Tzu

The Automatic Millionaire Homeowner by David Bach

Beware the Naked Man Who Offers You His Shirt by Harvey Mackay

Career Match: Connecting Who You Are with What You'll Love to Do by Shoya Zichy

Creating and Motivating a Superior, Loyal Staff by National Institute of Business Management

The Directory of Executive Recruiters by Kennedy Publications

Getting Things Done by David Allen

Good to Great by Jim Collins

How to Sell Anything to Anybody by Joe Girard

In Search of Excellence by Tom Peters

Knock 'Em Dead by Martin Yate

Lions Don't Need to Roar by D.A. Benton

The One Minute Manager by Kenneth Blanchard, PhD, and Spencer Johnson, MD

A Passion for Excellence by Tom Peters and Nancy Austin

Peak Performers by Charles Garfield

Rites of Passage at $100,000+ by John Lucht

Science of Getting Rich, The by Wallace D. Wattles

Success Secrets by Mark McCormack

Talk Your Way to the Top by Kevin Hogan

Think and Grow Rich (original 1937 version) by Napoleon Hill— this one is so good I have to list it again!

Warren Buffett Speaks by Janet Lowe

The Warren Buffett Way by Robert Hagstrom

What They Don't Teach You at Harvard Business School by Mark McCormack

Acknowledgments

First and foremost, I am eternally grateful to God—my Creator and Co-Creator. I am astounded by the perfect universe You have created for everyone. Your unconditional love leaves me in constant awe. Thank You for patiently prodding me to finally finish this book.

My mother and father were both English majors in college, so I guess I was programmed and destined to "read and write." I did both. I am grateful for the inspiration that you both gave me over the years. My mother introduced me to my mystical side with the book *Inner Skiing* and so many other books afterward; my father inspired me to excel in school even when I wanted to be a "dumb jock." I could not have written *The Bliss List* without their love, support, and patience.

To M.A.H.—the love of my life. Her love, support, and guidance are truly amazing. She is my inspiration and has taught me so many beautiful lessons.

To my children: Paul, Chris, and Jackie. May you follow your bliss and inspire your children to follow their bliss.

To my clients: I couldn't have become financially independent enough to write this book without your business. Thank you for your confidence in me. To my candidates: One of my greatest joys is to help you find bliss in your occupations. I am a better person because of you.

To Lisa Pelto, Ellie Pelto, and Erin Pankowski at Concierge Marketing, and Sandra Wendel. The first edition would not have won four awards without you. Also, thanks to Elaine Johnson, my favorite grammarian; Bob Condello for your creative and practical guidance; Meredith, a great mentor and friend.

Thanks to my literary agent Linda Konner. Your professional tenacity helps spread bliss throughout the world.

Finally, thanks to Senior Editor, Andrea Au Levitt, for believing in this book right from the start, and then helping to improve it.

About the Author

"The Ambassador of Bliss"

J. P. Hansen is an award-winning, bestselling author of three books, a professional speaker, and a life coach. In addition, he is CEO of an executive search company, and for the past twenty years, he has helped thousands of people find their dream jobs. A self-made millionaire at a young age, prior to founding his own business, he was the youngest vice president of sales & marketing at a Fortune 30 company (ConAgra). Previously, he successfully ascended the corporate ladders at blue-chip companies Nestle, SC Johnson Wax, and Bristol-Myers Squibb. He graduated from Boston College with a BA in English and an area of concentration in Economics.

Since January 2010, *The Bliss List* and *The Bliss List Journal* have garnered four awards (two international), including:

- ForeWord Book of the Year Medalist

- Career Book of the Year Award winner (Next Generation)

- Excellence Award national finalist (Indie)

- USA Book News Award national finalist

His novel, *Pink Slips and Glass Slippers*, became the #1 most downloaded book in the world on Amazon within its first month in October 2012, and continues at or near the top in most rankings.

J.P. has appeared live as a career expert, reaching over 15,000,000 people on national TV like FoxNews, Daytime TV, CBS, ABC, NBC, and FOX affiliates, on numerous radio programs in top markets, and in publications like the *Los Angeles Times*, *Fortune*, AOL, CareerBuilder, CNN.com, and FoxBusiness.com. *Omaha Magazine* dubbed J.P. "The Ambassador of Bliss."

For updates, visit www.BlissList.com and click "Like" on his author Facebook page: J.P. Hansen.

Index